WINRATE IS OVERRATED

A PRACTICAL GUIDE TO THINK LIKE A PROFESSIONAL TRADER

WITH VISUAL FRAMEWORKS & REFERENCE TABLES

BY

AJAS S

This book is intended for educational and informational purposes only.
The author does not provide financial, investment, or trading advice.
Trading involves risk, and readers are advised to exercise their own judgment and consult appropriate professionals before making any financial decisions.

Some illustrations in this book are generated using AI tools and have been curated and refined by the author.

Book Title: *WIN RATE IS OVERRATED*
ISBN: 978-93-5777-866-4
First Edition: 2026
Published by: Ajas S
Printed in: INDIA, US & UAE

FOREWORD

Walk into any bookstore, and you will find shelves lined with volumes on fundamental analysis, technical analysis, and trading psychology. What you rarely find is a guide that takes a trader by the hand and walks them from their very first trade to the peak of mastery.

There are countless factors beyond fundamentals, technicals, and psychology that typically take decades for a trader to fully grasp. In this book, **Ajas** covers those elusive areas, providing step-by-step guidance to take an amateur from novice to professional, and ultimately, to a maestro.

The industry has plenty of professionals, but very few true maestros. Mastery demands years of relentless, structured dedication. With this book, a master extends a hand to the amateur, offering a rare opportunity to drastically shorten the learning curve to success.

-SHIJUMON ANTONY
DERIVATIVES TRADER

CONTENTS

AUTHOR'S NOTE

When I started trading, I was chasing charts, not character.

I thought the next indicator, the next setup, or the next mentor would finally make me consistent.

But every time I made money, I lost peace.

And every time I lost money, I lost myself a little more.

Then one day, I realized something that changed everything:

The market isn't punishing you. It's reflecting you.

Every fear, every impulse, every ounce of greed I carried inside, the market mirrored it back to me.

And until I learned to master that reflection, no strategy could save me.

That realization became the seed for **WIN RATE IS OVERRATED**.

This book was born from years of mistakes, real losses, real emotions, real silence.

This book was written over nearly two years through bull runs, sharp corrections, and dramatic reversals.

When I began drafting it, gold was trading near $2,000. By the time these pages were refined, it had crossed $5,000 and now retraced to $4500 mark. Silver witnessed steep declines of nearly 30% within short spans.

Markets moved. Emotions shifted. Narratives changed.

The principles inside this book did not.

It's not written from theory, but from experience that broke me, rebuilt me, and finally set me free.

I've seen what happens when traders succeed too early and fail too soon.

I've seen what money can do when it arrives before maturity, and how losses can teach what success never could.

This book is for every trader who's felt that frustration, the kind that keeps you staring at a screen long after the candles have stopped moving. It's for the ones who've whispered, "Maybe this isn't for me" and yet still opened the charts again the next morning.

Because that's what traders do.

We fall. We learn. We adapt. And through it all, we grow.

WIN RATE IS OVERRATED isn't about strategies.

It's about survival, self-awareness, and the slow, quiet evolution of a human being who refuses to give up on mastery.

It's a reflection of every sleepless night, every emotional breakdown, every small moment of breakthrough that made me realize, the goal isn't to trade perfectly. The goal is to trade peacefully.

And if this book can save even one trader from emotional burnout, if it can make one person pause before revenge-trading, if it can remind one reader that consistency matters more than intensity, then the entire journey was worth it.

Some ideas may appear more than once throughout this book. This repetition is intentional, because mastery is built through reinforcement.

Thank you for letting me share this with you. I hope these pages bring you what the market could never give, peace, clarity, and control over yourself.

Because the greatest profit, you'll ever make…is the peace you feel when the chart stops defining your worth.

-Ajas S

ACKNOWLEDGMENTS

To every trader who ever lost money but refused to lose heart, this book is yours. To my mentors, peers, and friends who taught me humility and hunger, your lessons built the foundation beneath every page.

To my wife, **Dr. Sana Sainudeen**, my greatest supporter, thank you for understanding my passion, giving me space when I needed silence, and believing in me when I doubted myself. Your strength and faith helped me grow not only as a trader, but as a person.

To my parents, **M Sunil & Beegum N**, for always encouraging me to chase my dreams. To my in-laws, **Sainudeen AK & Saleena S**, for embracing me with faith and acceptance. And to our family members- thank you for unwavering support throughout this journey.

A special thanks to **Mr. ShijuMon Antony**, my first mentor, who guided me when I knew nothing about the markets and helped build the foundation I stand on today. His continued support, his willingness to review this book, and the thoughtful feedback he provided, along with writing the foreword, mean more to me than words can truly express.

To my friends and everyone I've met along the way, thank you for every conversation, perspective, and reminder that trading is only one part of a much larger life. Special mention to Subi, Shaffin, Anish, Gino, Akhil PL, Jineesh, Ajay, Adheel, Stanly and the many traders I met along the way.

To the trading community, authors, educators, and content creators who made knowledge accessible: thank you. Traders like **Subasish Pani**, **Sharique Shamsudeen**, and **Umar Ashraf**, and podcasts such as **Words of Rizdom** and **Titans of Tomorrow**, have shaped countless learners through generosity and insight.

Even to the pretenders I encountered, those who claimed to always time the market, I extend gratitude. You sharpened my judgment and pushed me toward real wisdom which ultimately became the core reason for writing this book.

Finally, to the markets themselves, thank you for being the most brutal, honest and transformative teacher I have ever known. The markets made me humbler, more disciplined, and more resilient.

PREFACE

Trading isn't just about charts, candlesticks, or indicators.

It's about the human mind, how it reacts, adapts, and sometimes breaks under pressure.

I've seen brilliant people fail because they couldn't manage emotion, and ordinary people succeed because they mastered patience.

We all start the same way, excited, curious, a little naive.

We think success is about learning strategies, finding the best entry, or predicting the next move.

But after years in the market, one truth becomes painfully clear:

You don't trade the market, you trade yourself.

That's what this book is about.

This isn't a guide to get rich quick.

It's a journey, from confusion to clarity, from chaos to calm.

It's the story of two people: **the Amateur**, who represents every trader's starting point, and **the Pro**, who represents the voice of experience, calm, detached, and quietly wise.

Their conversations are the essence of every lesson I wish someone had told me when I began.

This book isn't about trading perfectly, it's about becoming profitable, patient, and peaceful.

Because the truth is simple:

In trading, perfection is overrated. Consistency is freedom.

And win rate?

"WIN RATE IS OVERRATED"

ABOUT THE CHARACTERS

The "**Pro**" and the "**Amateur**" in this book are fictional representations.

The **Pro** in this book is not a single individual. He is a refined voice, shaped by years of observation, learning, and reflection.

His thinking is deeply inspired by my mentor, **Mr. Shijumon Antony**, whose insights, live trading sessions, and real-time decision-making played a foundational role in shaping my understanding of the markets. I spent months observing not just his trades, but more importantly, his mindset, his patience, and the way he approached uncertainty.

At the same time, the Pro is also an accumulation of wisdom gathered from countless hours of learning from experienced traders, interviews, discussions, and market participants across the world.

This book does not represent or claim the views of any one individual in isolation. Instead, it is a synthesis of ideas, experiences, and lessons that consistently appeared across different successful traders.

The **Amateur** represents all of us, including myself, at different stages of the journey.

If you see yourself in the Amateur, that is intentional.

The Pro represents what we can become. If you recognize wisdom in the Pro, it likely came from many disciplined minds before mine.

INTRODUCTION

Every trader starts the same way.

We open our first chart and feel a rush. Lines, patterns, indicators, all whispering possibility.

We make our first win and feel invincible. Then we take our first loss, and feel broken.

What follows is a loop of obsession, strategy-hopping, emotional swings, and endless learning.

We're told to **"cut losses quickly and let winners run,"**

but no one tells us **how** to actually do that when our hearts are racing and money is on the line.

We think we need more knowledge. But what we really need is more clarity.

The truth is, the market doesn't care how much you know.

It only rewards how well you can control yourself when things stop going your way.

This book is divided into five parts. Each representing a different layer of the trader's evolution:

The Journey Through This Book

Part I: Getting Started: The Amateur's World

- Where excitement meets illusion.
- The Amateur chases shortcuts, indicators, and perfection, until he confronts the uncomfortable truth that early wins don't equal skill.

Part II: The Trader's Edge

- Structure replaces speculation.

- The Pro introduces expectancy, probability, and risk control, showing that survival and consistency matter more than being right.

Part III: The Market's Reality

- Randomness becomes the teacher.
- The Amateur learns that traps, volatility, liquidity, and emotional swings aren't manipulation, they are structural components of the market.

Part IV: Path to Profitability

- Discipline replaces impulse.
- Here the focus shifts from ideas to execution, equity curve realism, scaling maturity, attention control, structured challenges, and non-negotiable routines that transform behaviour into consistency.

Part V: Trading Philosophy

- The final evolution.
- The trader understands that markets cannot be conquered only respected.

He stops chasing certainty and learns to coexist with uncertainty. Throughout the book, you'll see their world unfold like a dialogue, not a lecture, but a living mentorship. Every page combines **conversation**, **Visuals**, and **reflection**, so you don't just read the lessons, you feel them.

This isn't a technical manual. It's a mirror. A mirror that will quietly show you how your own thoughts shape your trading life. And when you finish, you won't just understand trading better, you'll understand yourself better

A NOTE TO THE READER

Dear Reader,

This book isn't meant to be read like a textbook.
It's meant to be experienced.

Take your time. Pause after each chapter.

Reflect on the Amateur's words, because they might sound like your own.

And absorb the Pro's insights, because they come from experience that can save you years of pain.

You might find yourself reading a line and feeling seen, as if the book is describing your current trading life.

That's by design. Because every trader, no matter how unique their path, fights the same battles.

Here's how to get the most out of this book: **Don't rush.** The Pro's lessons are layered. Read them like conversations, not commands.

Journal your reflections. After each chapter, note what part of you resonated or resisted.

Revisit later. Some lessons will make sense only after you've lived them.

Remember, every trader starts as the Amateur.

The goal is not to skip that phase, but to grow through it. If you ever find yourself lost in the market, come back to these pages. They're not written to impress you; they're written to remind you: You don't need to win every trade. You just need to protect your peace, follow your process, and let your edge play out. May this book be your quiet reset button when chaos surrounds you.

May it remind you that **the real trade is between you and yourself.** And when you finally find that balance, the market will start to feel like what it truly is: a mirror, not a battlefield.

-Ajas S

WHAT THIS BOOK IS NOT

Before you continue, let's clarify something important.

This book is not a strategy manual.

You will not find secret indicators, proprietary setups, or entry tricks hidden between these pages. The market does not reward secrets. It rewards structure.

This book is not a signal service.

No one here will tell you where to buy, where to sell, or how to "time the exact top." If someone consistently claims they catch every move from bottom to top, they are either extraordinary beyond probability, or they are selling certainty in a world governed by randomness.

This book is not a get-rich system.

Trading can create wealth, but only through patience, discipline, and survival. Anyone promising rapid multiplication without emotional cost is either inexperienced or dishonest.

This book is not a promise.

It does not guarantee profits. It does not eliminate drawdowns. It does not remove uncertainty.

What it offers is a framework.

A way to think. A way to behave. A way to survive long enough for your edge to compound.

If you are looking for shortcuts, this book will disappoint you.

If you are looking for structure, this book may change your trading forever.

PART 1: HOW AMATEURS THINK & ACT

"You don't learn the market by watching price move.
You learn it by watching yourself react."

1.1 THE BEGINNER'S DELUSION

"You made money, that doesn't mean you've beaten the market consistently."

Opening Scene

Amateur: "Pro, I made money in the last bull run. I turned $5k into $20K. Why does everyone say 90% of traders lose money? I'm thinking of quitting my job and trading full-time."
Pro: "First, congratulations on the win. Second, a single/few wins doesn't rewrite probability. That's where the trouble starts."

The Illusion of Early Wins

Pro: "Most beginners who post profits did two things: they were lucky because market conditions favoured them (a bull run, trending instrument), and they didn't risk real capital or responsibility. You caught a wave. That's different from learning to surf every sea."

Amateur: "Is this the reason why 90% lose money in the market?"

Pro: "The statistical headline of '90% lose' is blunt but it points to patterns: small capital, oversized expectations, no rules, and no safety net. Those four things destroy accounts faster than strategy weaknesses do."

A Personal Confession

Pro paused for a moment. "Let me tell you something," he said.

"There was a time I made money quickly during a strong bull run. It felt effortless. Every dip I bought worked. Every breakout continued. I thought I had cracked the code. But the market wasn't rewarding skill. It was rewarding momentum. When conditions changed, my confidence didn't. I continued the same aggression and slowly, the market took back what it had given.

That's when I understood something brutal: A rising market hides your weaknesses."

Why Small Money + Big Dreams = Fast Ruin

Pro: "Think of starting a small grocery shop. You need seed capital, time, customers, and learning. In trading, people treat it like a lottery ticket. They show up with $1,000 and dream of $100,000. That forces them to risk too much, too soon."

Amateur: "But I turned small into big, doesn't that prove it's possible?"

Pro: "Possible, yes. Repeatable, NO. If you risk everything on a single trade to turn small capital into a windfall, you're gambling, not operating a business."

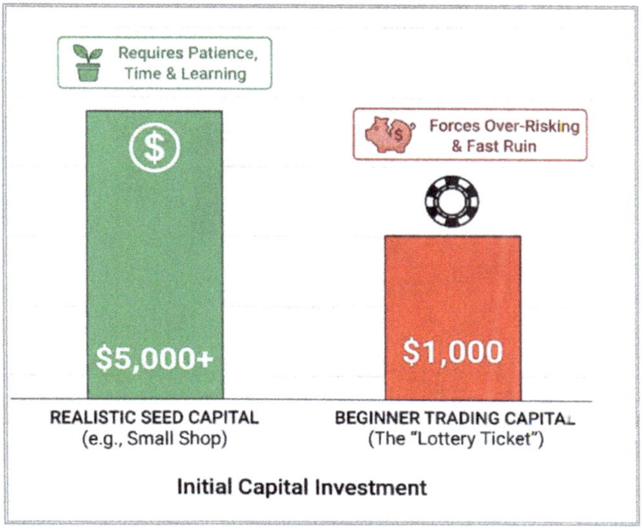

The Playground Problem, No Referee, No Rules

Pro: "In normal professions you train, apprentice, and pass exams. In a market playground, there is no referee. If you have money you can play, and many never learn the rules of money management before they risk it."

Pro: "That lack of referee + access to leverage = wild behaviour. People over-leverage, revenge trade, and refuse to accept small losses until the losses are catastrophic."

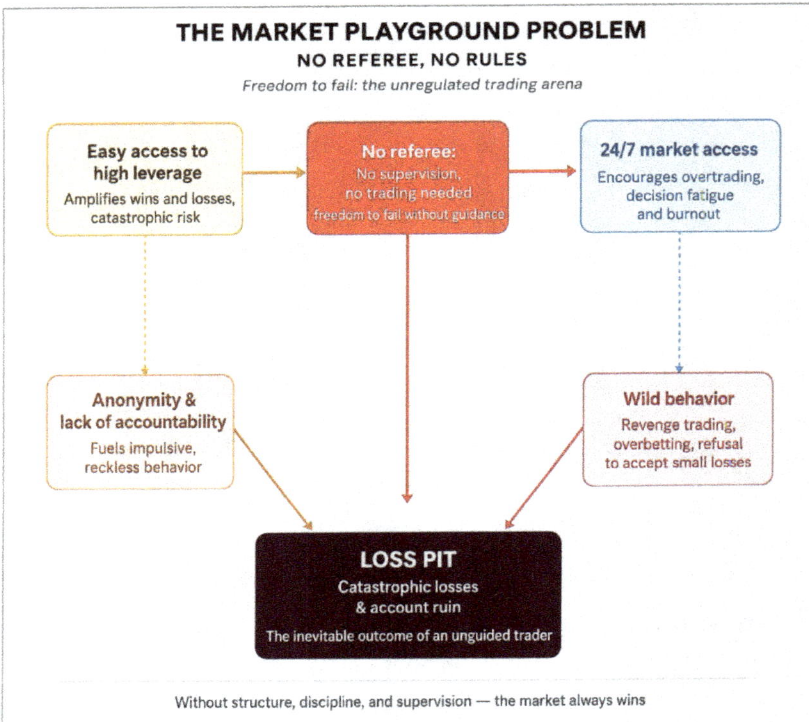

Expectations vs Reality, The Return Illusion

Pro: "Real investors expect 10–15% annually from disciplined investments. A high-performing business returning 20% is exceptional. Trading is not a legal way to multiply tiny capital into fortunes overnight; it's a skill that can produce superior returns **over time**, with discipline."

Pro: "If your expectation is monthly 50–100% because you once had a lucky run, that expectation will force reckless behaviour."

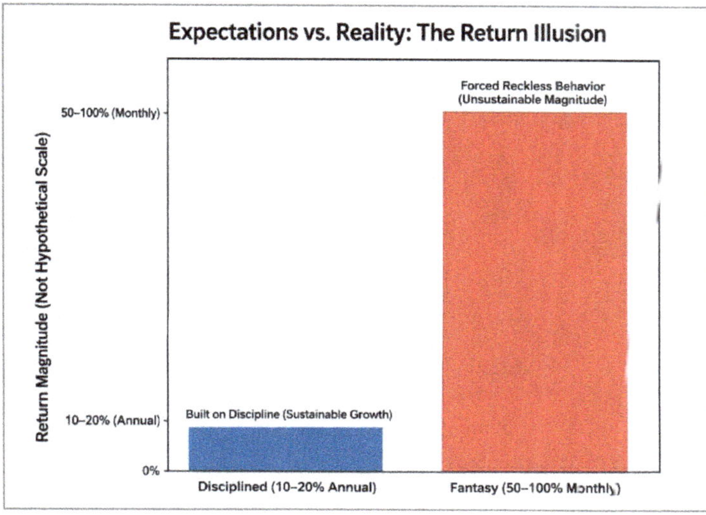

The Eggs & Basket Rule, Capital Preservation First

Pro: "Rule #1: Treat capital as ammunition. Rule #2: Don't put all your eggs in one trade. If you have 100 eggs, you can risk one egg many times. If you put all 100 in a single bet and lose, you have nothing left."

Practice- Start with survival-first money. Keep a steady income or buffer while you practice until you can show consistent results across market conditions.

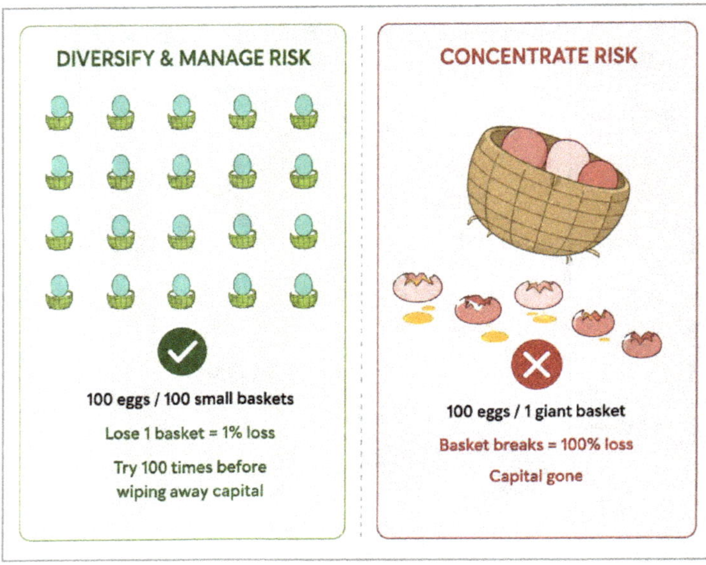

How to Move From "I was lucky" → "I'm a trader"

Pro: "There are three crucial shifts you must make before thinking of full-time trading."

1. **Expectation adjustment**: Set realistic targets (e.g., learn, then aim for low single-digit monthly returns that compound).
2. **Capital adequacy**: Have enough capital so risk per trade is small relative to living needs. If you must pay bills with trading, pressure ruins decisions.
3. **Process & proof**: Show consistent positive expectancy over a statistically meaningful sample (50–100 trades, by your given timeframe).

Amateur: "What if I want to speed up?"
Pro: "You don't. Speed destroys repeatability. Slow compounding and process stability build careers."

The Modern Safety Tools (short preview)

Pro: "There are modern ways to scale without giving your life savings to the market: funded accounts (Prop Firms), part-time trading while you keep MAIN income, and structured risk-limited experiments. Use them as discipline engines, not tickets."

"A single win is a headline. Consistency is a career."

Final Reflection

Amateur: "So making money once doesn't make you ready."
Pro: "Exactly. The market rewards survival more than genius. If you survive the early years, you give your edge time to compound."

Chapter Summary

• Early wins often come from favourable conditions, not repeatable skill.
• Small capital + large expectations is the fastest route to ruin.
• Trading lacks external referees. Discipline must be internalized.
• Treat capital as ammunition; diversify risk (don't put all eggs in one trade).
• Survive first; scale later. Prove consistency across many trades, weeks, months, quarters & years.
• Use modern discipline tools (Prop firms, funded challenges, steady income) as accelerators, not shortcuts.

1.2 WHY THIS BOOK EXISTS

The Real Purpose: Becoming Profitable, Not Perfect

Opening Scene

Amateur: "Pro, I've watched videos, bought courses, and studied every indicator. Yet I keep losing money. What am I missing?"

Pro: "You're missing the point. Trading isn't about knowing everything, it's about mastering the few things that matter. The goal isn't to be perfect; it's to be profitable."

Pro (smiling): "You've already faced the first truth of trading we discussed last time; it's not about early wins or lucky streaks; it's about survival and repetition.
Most traders step into the market chasing excitement and end up meeting reality. Now that your expectations are grounded, it's time to build structure, to understand what really keeps a trader consistent."

Pro: "Let's move from randomness to rhythm. You don't need more information; you need a framework that keeps you disciplined."

Amateur: "So the problem isn't that I don't know enough, it's that I don't apply enough?"

Pro: "Exactly. The market doesn't reward effort; it rewards execution. In this chapter, we'll start laying the foundation, how to focus on what matters, create balance between risk and reward, and build the kind of process that protects you when luck runs out."

Every Trader Knows the Theory, Few Live It

Pro: "Everyone knows the rule: cut losses quickly, let winners run. But theory dies the moment emotion enters the trade."

He smiled.

Pro: "The market doesn't test your knowledge. It tests how long you can stay rational while money moves."

Why This Book Exists

Pro: "This book isn't about predicting markets or finding secret setups.

It's about teaching the Amateur how to survive long enough to become profitable."

Amateur: "So it's like learning to ride a bike?"

Pro: "Exactly. First you balance. Then you ride.

Only after you're stable can you try stunts. But, you still can fall and it could be fatal as well"

The Learning Curve Every Trader Faces

Pro: "When traders start, they commit four common mistakes."

Mistake	Description
No System	**Jumping** between indicators & opinions.
No Risk Control	Betting too large, **hoping** instead of planning.
No Journaling	Repeating errors, forgetting context.
No Patience	Expecting mastery before repetition.

Pro: "Amateurs seek certainty. Pros build consistency.

You don't need a perfect system; you need a repeatable one."

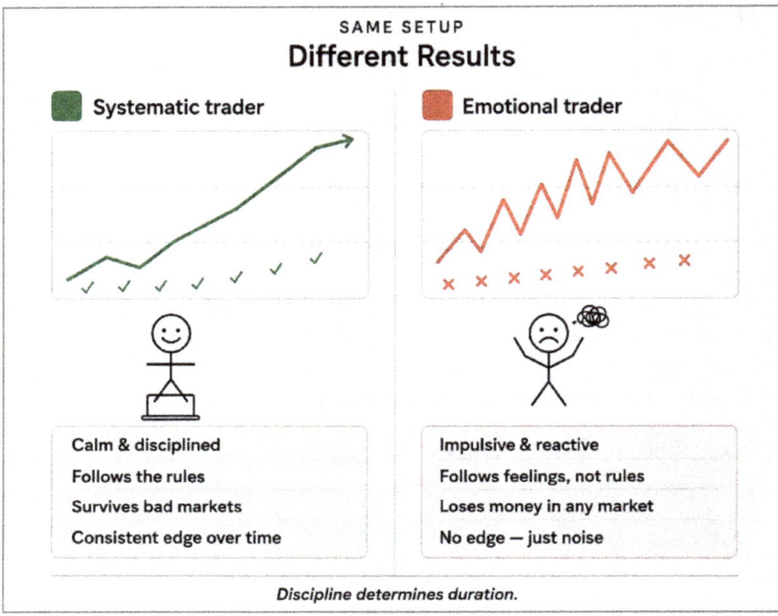

System vs Strategy

Amateur: "But aren't systems and strategies the same?"

Pro: "A strategy tells you when to enter. A system tells you how to behave. One makes you money in good markets. The other keeps you alive in bad ones. That's why even with the same setup, two traders get opposite results, one follows a system, the other follows feelings."

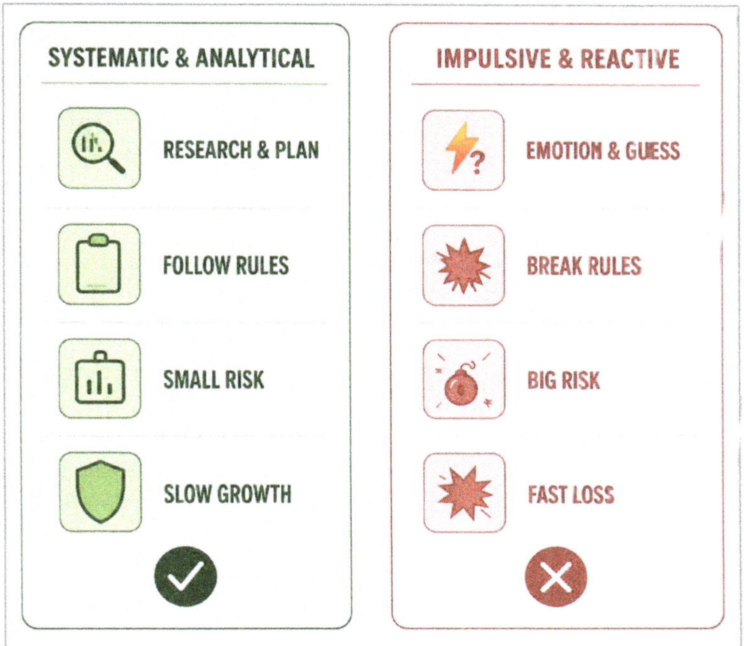

The Strategy Collector Phase

Pro smiled.

"I've been there too, thinking strategies are everything. Moving averages. RSI. Bollinger Bands. Heiken Ashi. Volume spikes. Fair Value Gaps. Every month, a new system. For a short time, each one worked. Then it failed. The truth was not that the indicators were broken. The truth was that I was unstable.

When you change systems every time you lose, you are not refining, you are escaping."

The Market's True Nature

Pro: "Markets rise and fall because people think differently at the same moment.

One person buys believing price will rise; another person sells believing it will fall.

That tension creates movement."

He continued, "You can't time every move.

There are too many participants, funds, banks, retail, algos, all acting on their own logic.

Trying to out-guess them is like trying to predict what everyone at a dinner table will say next."

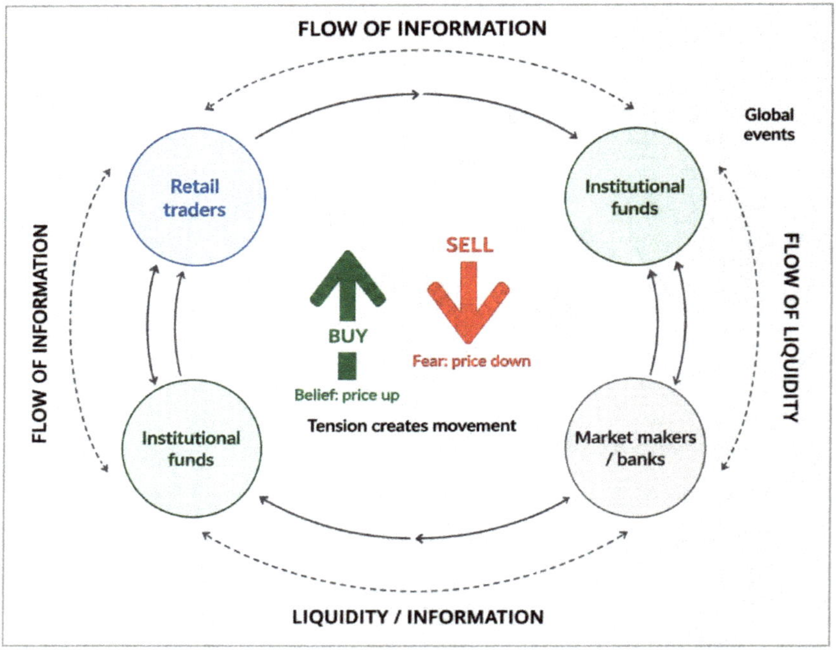

Anything Can Happen at Any Time

Pro: "In trading, certainty is an illusion. Think of flipping a coin. Heads = win, Tails = loss. Each toss is random, but over a hundred flips, patterns emerge." He sketched a quick chart on paper.

Pro: "That's how professionals think, in probabilities, not predictions."

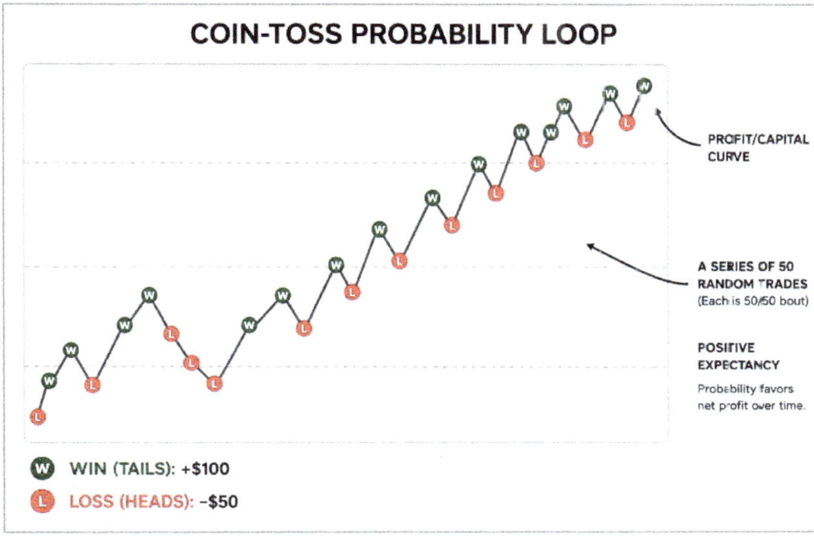

Why Most Traders Fail

Pro: "Not because they lack information. They fail because they want control in a place built on uncertainty."

He leaned forward.

Pro: "Remember this, you can't control outcome, but you can control exposure."

"Control exposure, not outcome."

"Once you learn to manage risk mathematically and emotions psychologically, profitability becomes a by-product of discipline."

The Purpose of This Book

Pro: "The Amateur in you wants excitement.

The Pro in you wants endurance.

This book is about bridging that gap." He smiled.

Pro: "You'll learn three pillars, the Trading Edge, the Mathematical Edge, and the Psychological Edge.

Master those, and you'll never depend on luck again."

"The market is not here to trick you. It's here to test you."

Final Reflection

Amateur: "So the real goal isn't to win every trade."

Pro: "No. The real goal is to trade long enough to discover who you become in the process."

Chapter Summary

- Every trader knows the rules, few live them.
- Consistency > Certainty.
- Systems sustain you when strategies fail.
- Markets move because beliefs collide.
- Think in probabilities, not predictions.
- Control exposure, not outcome.
- Profit is a result; peace is the reward.

1.3 UNDERSTANDING MARKET MOVEMENT

Why the Market Moves the Way It Does

Opening Scene

Amateur: "Pro, sometimes I feel the market is alive, like it's watching me.
Every time I buy, it falls. When I sell, it jumps back up. Is it hunting me?"

Pro: "No, it's not hunting you. It's just doing what it's supposed to do, moving between belief and disbelief."

The Market Is a Crowd, not a Machine

Pro: "Every tick on the screen is a human decision, fear, greed, reaction, prediction.
Put millions of those decisions together and you get the market."

He leaned forward.

"That's why the same chart looks bullish to one trader and bearish to another.
The market isn't logical, it's emotional mathematics."

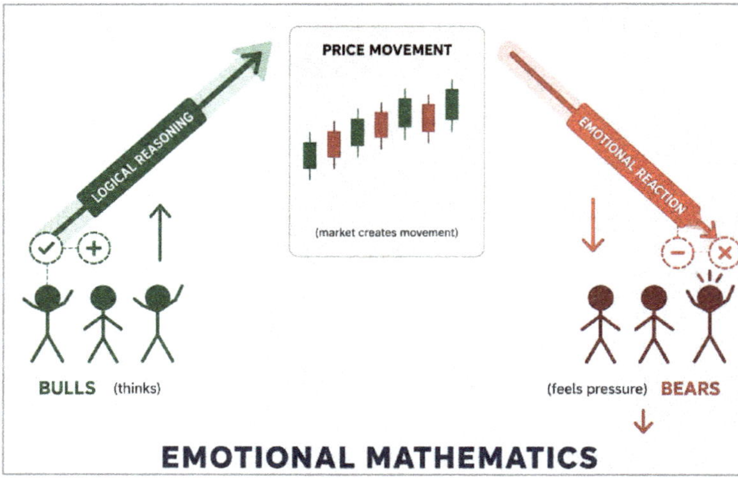

How the Market Breathes

Pro: "Think of the market like the ocean, tides and waves.
Liquidity flows in and out across time zones: Tokyo, London, New York.
Banks open, algos activate, traders wake up, each adding volume."

He drew a quick sketch.

"That's why price consolidates when liquidity is thin and expands when sessions overlap."

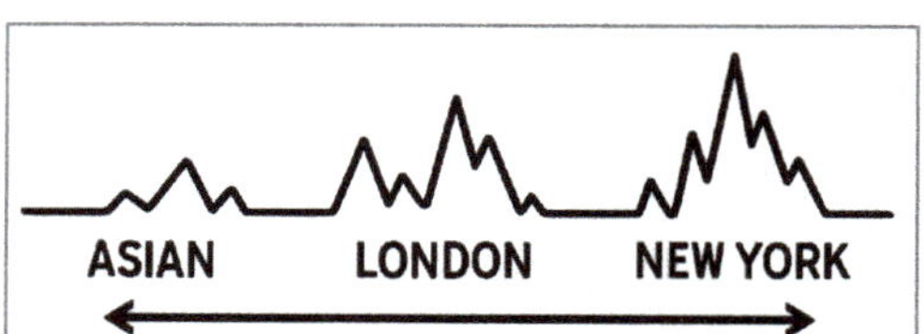

Why Price Moves Up and Down

Amateur: "So price rises when there are more buyers?"

Pro: "Not exactly. Price rises when buyers are more aggressive than sellers. It falls when sellers hit bids faster than buyers can absorb them."

He smiled.

"The market moves not because one side wins, but because one side gives up first."

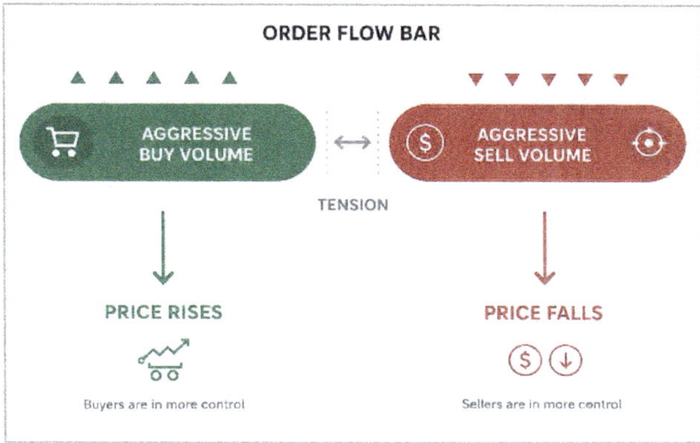

The Myth of Prediction

Pro: "The Amateur looks for certainty. The Professional looks for probability."

Amateur: "But can't technical analysis predict direction?"

Pro: "Technical analysis doesn't predict, it frames possibilities. Your job is to manage exposure when one of those possibilities plays out."

He paused.

"You don't forecast the storm; you build a house that survives it."

"You don't forecast the storm; you build a house that survives it."

The Trap of Confirmation

Pro: "When you want the market to confirm your bias, you start seeing what you want.
That's why most traders add more indicators, they're not seeking confirmation, they're seeking comfort."

Amateur: "So, indicators aren't useless, but my relationship with them is?"

Pro: "Exactly. Indicators are mirrors of price, not predictors of future."

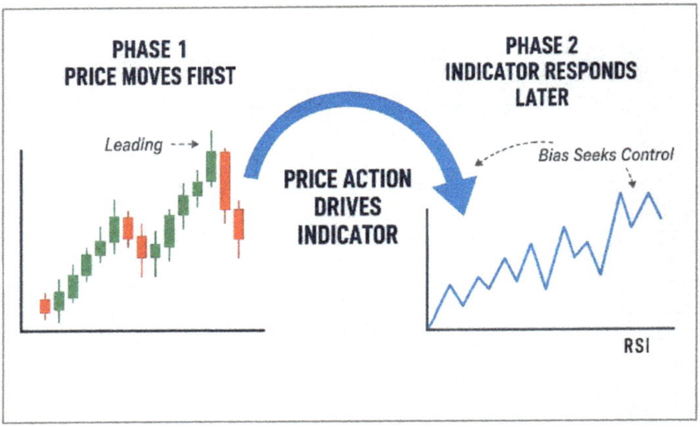

Liquidity and Traps

Pro: "Ever wondered why price often hits your stop before moving in your favour?
That's liquidity engineering, the market collecting orders before moving."

He drew two rectangles:

"Retail traders cluster stops below obvious lows or above visible highs. Institutions need those orders to fill large positions. The market dips there, fills them, and then runs."

Amateur: "So it's not manipulation, it's mechanics?"

Pro: "Precisely. The market hunts liquidity, not you."

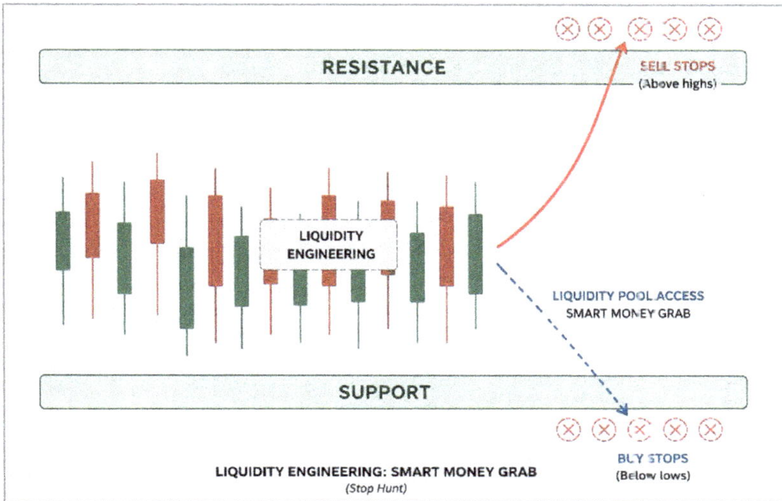

The Emotional Pattern of Every Cycle

Pro: "Every cycle follows the same emotional path. Once you recognize this rhythm, you stop chasing and start observing."

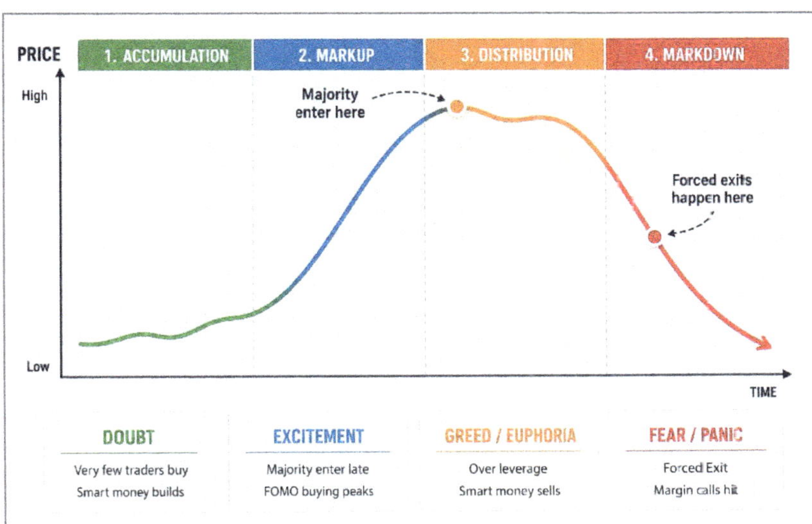

The Probability Mindset

Pro: "Remember the coin-toss example from before?

The market is the same game, just with better storytelling."

He scribbled on a pad.

"If you flip a fair coin a hundred times, results cluster randomly, but over time, the edge shows. Trading is just a hundred-coin tosses with controlled risk."

Amateur: "So a losing streak doesn't mean I'm wrong?"

Pro: "It means probability is doing its job. The key is to stay in the game long enough for math to work."

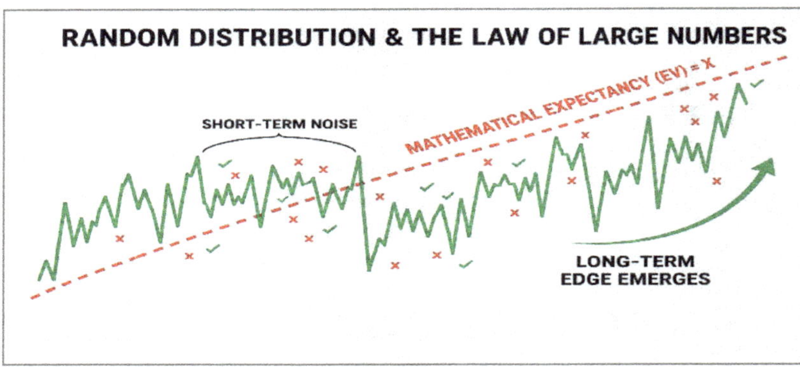

The Law of Opposing Beliefs

Pro: "Every trade exists because someone believes the opposite. For every buyer thinking it's going up, there's a seller believing it's going down. Both can be right, at different times."

Amateur: "So it's not about being right; it's about surviving the interval between wrong and right."

Pro: "Exactly."

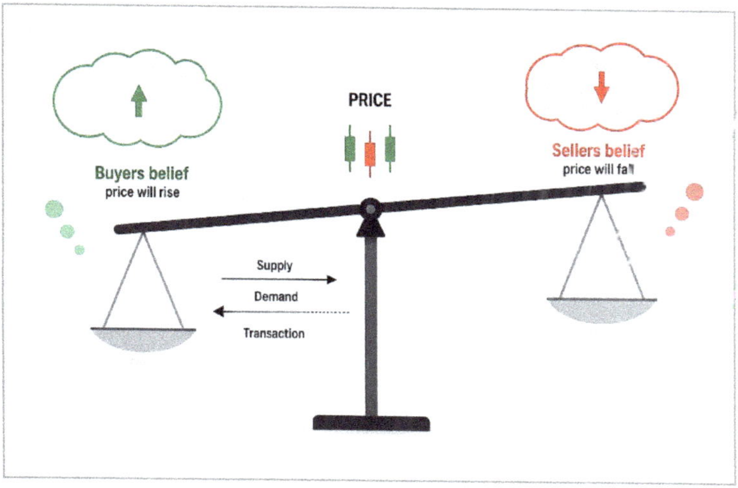

The Lesson

Pro: "The market isn't your enemy. It's a mirror showing you how impatient, fearful, or greedy you are. Once you understand its rhythm, it stops feeling random."

"The market doesn't move to punish you; it moves to educate you."

Final Reflection

Amateur: "So I can't control where the market goes, only how I respond."
Pro: "Exactly. The difference between chaos and clarity is the space between impulse and action."

Chapter Summary

- The market is a collective emotion, not a single force.
- Liquidity drives movement; timing sessions shape volatility.
- Price moves because one side gives up first.
- Indicators reflect, not predict.

- Liquidity grabs are mechanics, not malice.
- Emotional cycles repeat; awareness prevents entrapment.
- Probability is the only constant.
- Opposing beliefs create every trade, patience decides who profits.

1.4 THE SHORTCUT ILLUSION

"Mentors, Signals and The Danger of Perfect Marketing"

Opening Scene

Amateur: "Pro, I see so many mentors online. Some show luxury cars, some claim they catch every move, some say all their days are green. How do I know who's real?"

Pro paused. "I'm glad you asked that early. I didn't."

Pro Admits His Early Mistake

Pro: "When I started, I followed someone like that. He claimed he caught every major move. He posted screenshots of perfect entries. He said he had cracked the market. I believed him."

Amateur: "What happened?"

Pro: "It took time to realize the perfection was performance."

The Truth About Courses

Pro: "Let's be fair. There is nothing wrong with selling education. Every profession has teachers. A good mentor can save you years of trial and error. Learning from someone else's mistakes is smarter than burning your own capital repeatedly. The problem isn't courses. The problem is illusion."

The Red Flag That Should Scare You

Amateur: "What illusion?"

Pro: "Perfection. If someone says:

- I caught all the moves
- I rarely lose
- All my days are green
- I have a secret system

Be careful. No trader catches all moves. No trader avoids drawdowns. No trader wins daily. Markets are probabilistic. Not obedient."

The Mentor Collapse Story

Pro lowered his voice. "I once knew a trader who convinced many that he had found the holy grail.

He poached mentees from other groups. He mocked other mentors. He claimed superiority.

"People quit jobs because of him. Some stopped focusing on their main careers. Some sold profitable businesses. Some shifted to work-from-home roles to focus only on trading. They believed consistency was guaranteed.

At one stage, he was showcasing a lifestyle that appeared untouchable: modifying luxury cars worth 100,000-200,000 and posting from high-end apartments, investing lakhs into elaborate work setups, and upgrading gadgets effortlessly.

He publicly mocked established traders whenever they shared losing days, positioning himself as someone who never faltered.

He also built an image of strong ethics: openly criticizing piracy, even claiming he purchased the same course twice despite having access to unofficial recordings. These gestures were carefully displayed, reinforcing the narrative that he respected 'real work' and operated with integrity.

Everything contributed to a powerful projection: success, superiority, and moral credibility. And many believed it."

Amateur: "And then?"

Pro: "Over time, inconsistencies began to surface. His narratives didn't align. There was increasing pressure to enroll in higher-priced mentorships. More products were introduced: indicators, private groups, exclusive tools, all positioned as necessary for the next level. Questions started emerging. Some traders asked for long-term verified performance not screenshots, but sustained records.

There was resistance. Gradually, it became clear that the performance being projected was not supported by consistent profitability. The bold claims of making multiples beyond other mentors did not hold under scrutiny.

Exposure followed. Enrolments slowed. Revenue dried up. Financial obligations remained. Assets were sold. Lifestyle contracted. Appearances changed. He moved into a smaller apartment. Debt increased. At one point, even basic expenses became heavy. Trading didn't destroy him. Overconfidence and illusion did."

Pro paused. "But the real damage was not just financial. Many mentees had taken aggressive risks believing the illusion. Some borrowed. Some over-leveraged. Losses mounted. Confidence collapsed. Disappointment turned into depression for a few."

"Trading did not destroy them. Blind belief did."

Why People Fall for It

Pro: "Because easy money is attractive. Lifestyle marketing works. If someone shows cars, watches, beach-front apartments, people assume trading created it. But often the lifestyle is funded by enrolment fees. Students pay the EMI."

Signal Sellers

Amateur: "What about signal groups?"

Pro: "I don't support signal dependency."

- "Signals don't teach you:
- Why that entry works
- Where the stop-loss logic comes from
- How position size is calculated
- How to handle drawdown"

"You copy trades without understanding. When signals stop, your growth stops. Education builds independence. Signals build dependence."

How To Evaluate a Mentor Properly

Pro wrote down a checklist.

Ask these questions:

- ☐ Do they show multi-year performance?

- ☐ Do they openly discuss losing streaks?
- ☐ Do they teach risk before reward?
- ☐ Do they discourage over-leverage?
- ☐ Do they encourage you to build your own system?
- ☐ Do they show full statements, not cropped screenshots?
- ☐ Do they talk more about discipline than entries?

"If the answer to most of these is no," Pro said calmly, "walk away."

The Real Purpose of Mentorship

Amateur: "So should I never enroll?"

Pro: "Enroll to learn. Not to worship. Extract principles. Understand risk. Build your own framework. A good mentor wants you to outgrow him. If your mentor wants permanent dependence, that's not education. That's business."

Direct Confrontation of Fake Marketing

Pro leaned forward. "Here's the harsh truth."

"If someone truly understood the market deeply, they would not need to prove perfection daily. Real traders sell structure. Scammers sell speed. Real traders talk about survival. Scammers talk about luxury. Real traders respect uncertainty. Scammers promise control."

Final Reflection

Amateur: "So the danger isn't education. It's illusion."

Pro: "Exactly. The market is already hard. Don't let marketing make it harder. Seek transparency. Respect longevity. Avoid perfection. And remember: if someone says they caught every move…"

He smiled slightly. "…either they are God. Or they are lying."

Chapter Summary

- Education is not the enemy. Illusion is.
- Perfection claims are red flags.
- Lifestyle marketing is not proof of profitability.
- Multi-year consistency matters more than screenshots.
- Signals create dependence. Systems create independence.
- A true mentor builds your autonomy, not your addiction.

PART 2: THE TRADER'S EDGE

"You don't need to predict the market.
You just need an edge that survives uncertainty."

2.1 THE FIRST PILLAR: TRADING EDGE

How Professionals Think Differently

Opening Scene

Amateur: "Pro, everyone keeps talking about having an edge.
But what exactly is an edge? Is it a secret strategy? A rare setup?"

Pro: "No. An edge isn't what you see on the chart. It's what you do after you see it."

What an Edge Really Is

Pro: "An edge is any repeatable process that gives you a small advantage over randomness.
It doesn't guarantee profits every trade; it ensures consistency over many."

He drew two columns on paper:

No Edge (Random)	With Edge (Disciplined)
Random size per trade	Fixed/Defined risk per trade
Emotional entries	Systematic triggers
Cut winners early	Let winners breathe
Move stops randomly	Pre-defined exit logic

Pro: "An edge isn't magic; it's math and mindset working together."

The Coin Toss Experiment

Pro: "Imagine tossing a coin 100 times. Heads win $200, Tails lose $100. What happens after 100 tosses?"

Amateur: "Even with 50–50 chances, I'd still make money."

Pro: "Exactly. That's an edge. Not from prediction, from structure."

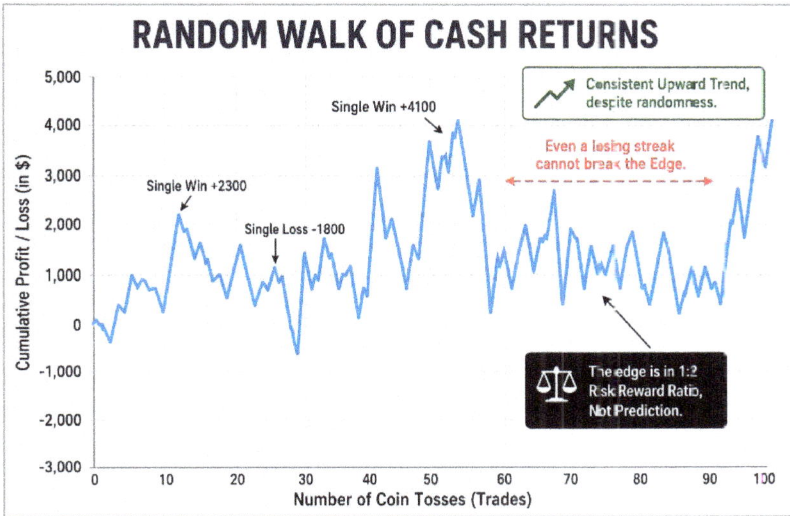

Pro: "Now replace the coin with your trades. It's not about being right. It's about being mathematically aligned."

Why 50% Accuracy Is Enough

Pro: "Most traders chase 90% accuracy. Professionals chase positive expectancy."

He wrote:

Expectancy = (Win% × Average Win) – (Loss% × Average Loss)

"Even with 50% wins, if your winners are twice your losers, you make money.
That's why pros can be wrong as often as they're right, and still be profitable."

The 4 Quadrants of Trading

Pro: "Every trade you take lands in one of four columns."

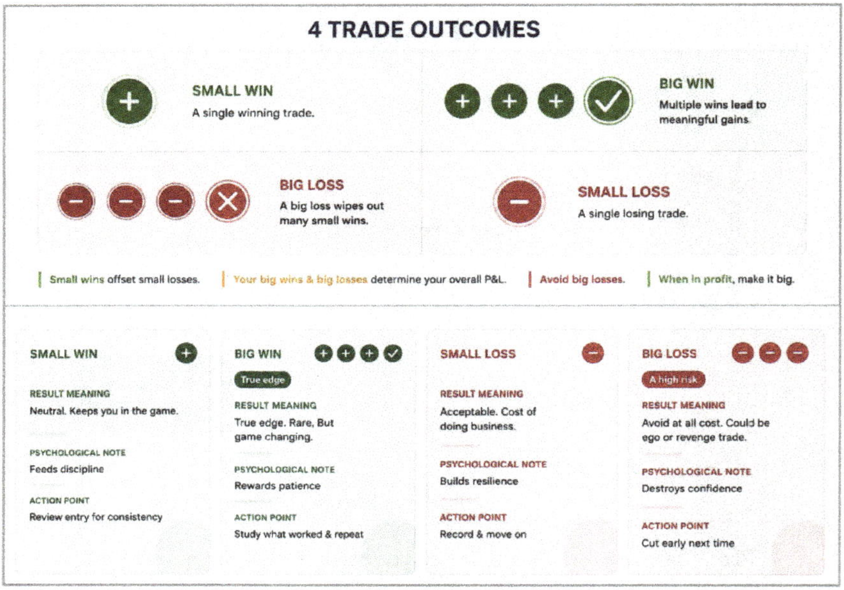

Pro: "Each quarter tells a clear story. Your entire job as a trader is to eliminate the Big Losses. Once that box disappears, profitability becomes inevitable."

Amateur: "So consistency isn't about more wins, it's about smaller mistakes."
Pro: "Exactly."

A Clarification on Big Winners

Amateur: "So to get big winners… should I increase my position size?"

Pro: "That's the most common misunderstanding. Big winners can come in two ways.

1. Large position size with small price movement.
2. Normal position size with large price movement."

He paused.

"Both can create big profits. But only one is sustainable."

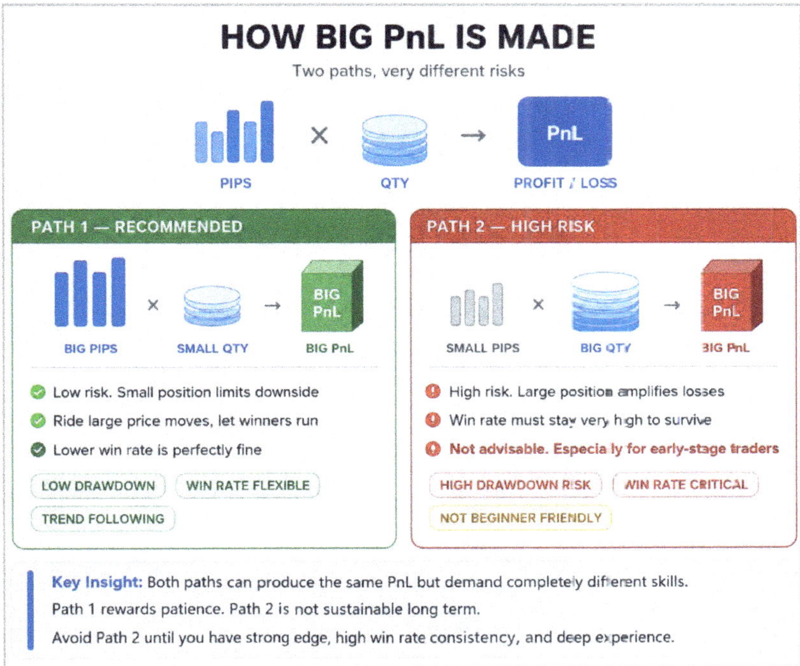

Pro continued: "When you rely on larger size…You're increasing risk, not edge. A small mistake can become a large loss. Professionals don't force big profits through size. They allow profits by holding the right trade."

"Big winners should come from movement… not size."

Pro: "If your growth depends on size, it's fragile. If it comes from holding quality trades, it's repeatable.

The small position sizes mentioned here are intended for safety and practice purposes. As we progress with trading and review the journal, we will determine the ideal position size."

The Edge Is Found in Repetition

Pro: "One trade means nothing. One hundred trades show everything. Every professional has hundreds of small trades behind every visible success. That's where probability gets enough data to reveal your real edge."

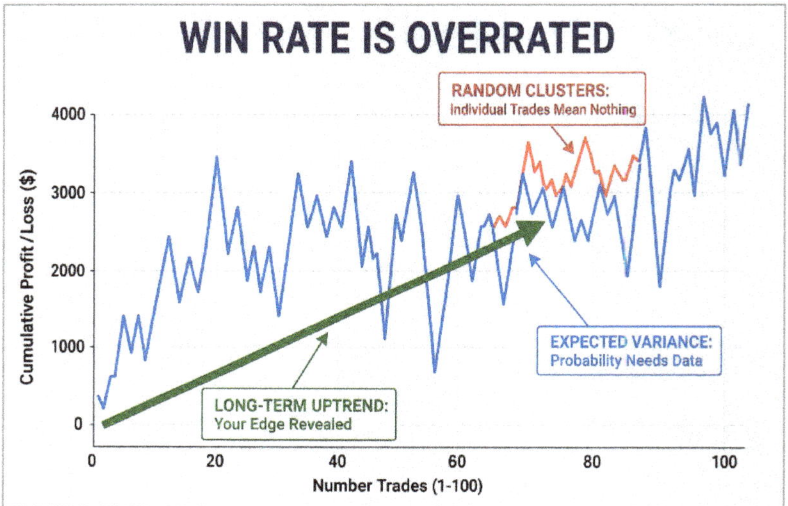

What Kills the Edge

Pro: "Three habits destroy your edge faster than any loss."

Mistake	Why It Hurts
Changing System Mid Trade	Breaks consistency, probability collapses
Over Sizing	One bad trade erases many good ones
Averaging	Adding to losing position converting small loser into big ones
Seeking Revenge Trades	Emotional trading replaces mathematical logic

Pro: "A single undisciplined day can undo a month of disciplined execution."

"A single undisciplined day can wipe out many days, weeks and sometimes months of profit."

The Edge Exists Only in Consistency

Amateur: "Pro, I understand strategy… but there are so many ways to manage a trade. Some use tight stop-loss, some use swing levels, some re-enter, some trail, some book partial profits. How do I know what's right?"

Pro: "That's the wrong question. It's not about what is right. It's about what is repeatable.

In trading, there are multiple ways to manage a position. Some traders use fixed risk (R-based stop-loss), some re-enter if the setup remains valid, some trail profits, some exit partially at key levels, and some use higher timeframe targets. All of these can work, but only under one condition, consistency.

If you apply one method today, another tomorrow, and something else next week, you don't have a system. You have randomness. An edge is not created by a single trade. It is created by repeating the same behaviour over a large number of trades. Your edge does not exist in your strategy. It exists in your consistency.

Most traders lose their edge because they change behaviour based on recent outcomes. After a loss, they tighten stop-loss. After missing a move, they hold longer. After seeing profits reverse, they exit early. That is not adaptation. That is emotional reaction.

You don't judge a method in 5 or 10 trades. You judge it over 100 or 150 trades. Only then does probability play out.

I'll give you a simple example. I held a position on a Friday. I had strong profits during the day, but I held on for a higher timeframe move. The market reversed, and the trade went from a large profit to a loss.

A few weeks later, under similar market conditions, I followed the same approach again. This time, I didn't react to the fear from the previous Friday's midday move. I stayed with my plan and held the trade without exiting on the dip.

The market eventually moved in my favour, and the trade delivered a much larger gain, nearly three times what I had seen earlier.

What I lost before was not only recovered, but exceeded. I didn't change my method. I stayed consistent.

Not because I was right that day… but because I was consistent across both days. Understand this clearly. One trader may exit early and re-enter to compound gains. Another may hold for large moves and accept drawdowns. Both can be profitable. Neither is right or wrong. It depends on how consistently they execute.

Think of a batsman. Rohit Sharma plays the pull shot and has been dismissed many times doing it. Virat Kohli plays the cover drive and has lost his wicket many times the same way. But they don't stop playing those shots. Over the long run, those are their strengths. They are not playing for one ball. They are playing for their career.

In trading, you are not judged by one trade. You are defined by your behaviour over time. If you keep changing your method based on recent outcomes, you destroy your edge. If you stay consistent, your edge reveals itself.

Consistency is not comfort. It is commitment to a process… even when outcomes fluctuate."

The amateur drifted into deep thoughts and filled pages with notes after the explanation. The Pro drank some water and watched the amateur writing notes.

Thinking in Series, Not Singles

Pro: "Amateurs judge performance by single trades. Pros judge by series of trades."

He smiled,

"Think of a cricketer, a century doesn't define his career; his batting average does."

Pro: "The same logic applies here; your average expectancy defines you."

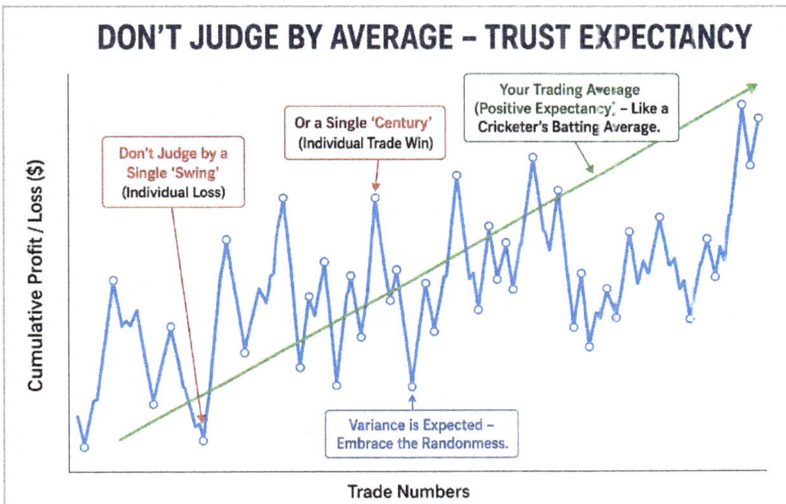

Your edge is invisible in one trade but undeniable over a hundred."

Final Reflection

Amateur: "So edge isn't about prediction. It's about how I handle uncertainty repeatedly."
Pro: "Exactly. The edge is a habit, not a hack."

Chapter Summary

- Edge = Repeatable advantage + disciplined execution.
- 50% accuracy is enough with 2:1 reward structure.
- Four Quadrants: **avoid big losses**, let big wins happen.
- Think in probabilities, not perfection.
- Edge appears over series, not single trades.
- The only real loss is breaking your own system.

2.2 THE SECOND PILLAR, MATHEMATICAL EDGE

How to Survive Long Enough for Probability to Work in Your Favor

Opening Scene

Amateur: "Pro, you always talk about probability and edge, but my problem isn't knowing the math. It's living it. Every time I try to calculate risk or reward, I end up reacting instead."

Pro: "That's because you think math is cold.
But in trading, math is mercy. It protects you from yourself."

The Law of Probabilities

Pro: "No system wins all the time. Every strategy has a random distribution of wins and losses. That means you can't judge a method by 3 trades or even 10."

He took out a sheet and wrote:

"If your system has 60% accuracy, that doesn't mean you'll win 6 out of every 10 trades. It means that over 100 trades, 60 will likely be winners, but not evenly spaced."

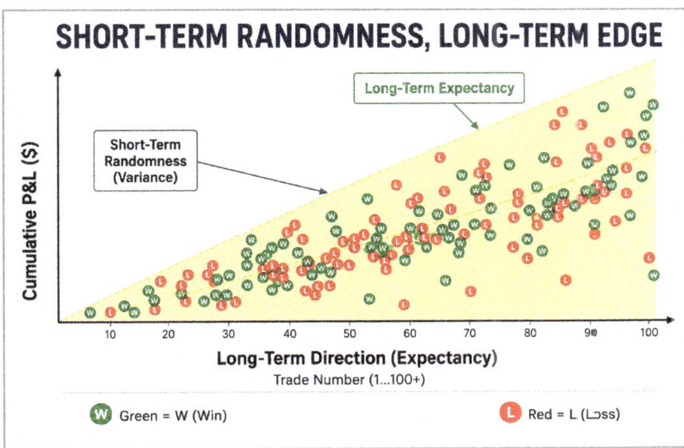

Pro: "Professionals expect variance; amateurs fight it.
The moment you accept randomness; you free yourself from overreaction."

The 4 Quadrants, Expanded

Pro: "Remember our four boxes from earlier?
Let's go deeper."

He drew four squares again.

Outcome Type	Meaning	Psychological Effect
Small Loss	Normal Business Cost. Part of the Game.	Builds resilience
Big Loss	Hidden Danger, Avoid at all cost.	Destroys confidence
Small Win	Controlled Profit. Keeps System alive.	Strengthens discipline
Big Win	True Edge. Rare but powerful.	Rewards patience & process

Pro: "The Pro's job is to operate without making big losses. Small Wins keep the system alive; Big Wins accelerate growth. Big Losses destroy the account, and Small Losses are the tuition you pay for experience. Remember, big losses can be a big losing trade, day, week or month"

Amateur: "So I can lose half my trades and still win overall, if I avoid the big losses."

Pro: "Exactly."

"Avoid big losses and aim to maximize the winner without increasing the risk. That's the real edge."

The Mathematics of Expectancy

Pro: "Let's make this real with numbers." He scribbled a simple formula:

Expectancy = (Win% × Average Win) – (Loss% × Average Loss)

Then filled it in:

Expectancy = (50% × \$2,000) – (50%× \$1,000) = \$500 per trade on average

"It means if you take 100 trades, you expect to earn \$50,000, provided you stay consistent and risk the same percentage each time."

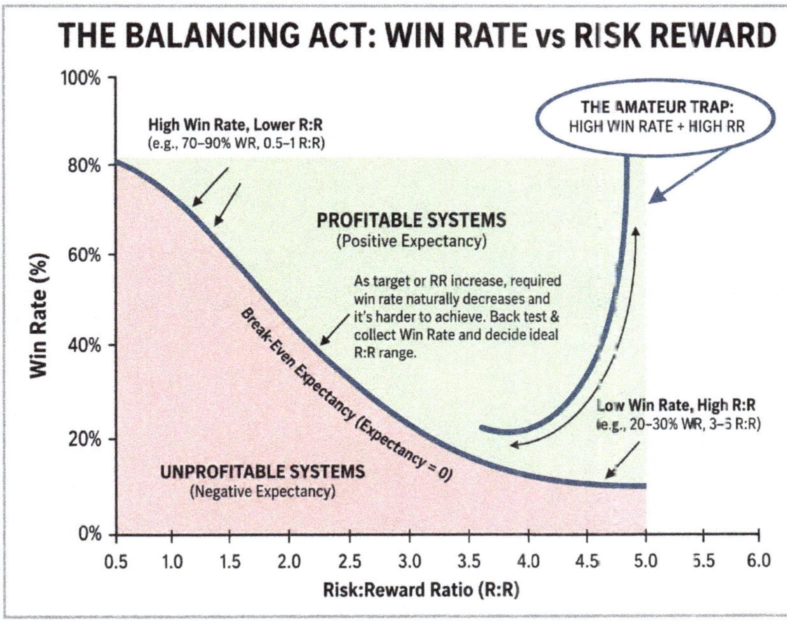

Pro: "Expectancy doesn't care about emotion; it only cares about consistency."

Position Sizing, The Real Secret of Longevity

Amateur: "Everyone says risk management is important, but what does it really mean in numbers?"

Pro: "Simple, never risk more than a small, fixed percentage of your capital on any trade."

He drew another example:

Account	Risk %	Amount per Trade
$10,000	1%	$100
$50,000	1%	$500
$100,000	1%	$1000

Pro: "That's how professionals think.
They size risk, not emotion. A small loss hurts the ego but protects the account."

The Hidden Enemy, Compounding Drawdown

Pro: "Most traders forget this; a 50% drawdown needs a 100% gain to recover." He wrote quickly:

Drawdown	Recovery Needed
10%	11%
25%	33%
50%	100%
75%	300%

Pro: "That's why I say, protect capital first, grow later. Compounding works both ways: up or down."

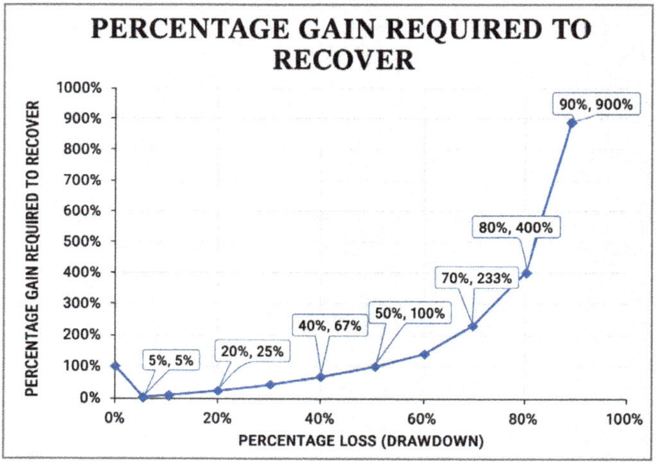

The Risk of Ruin

Pro: "Even a strong system can fail if position size is wrong. The risk of ruin is the probability your account will hit zero before your edge plays out."

Amateur: "So how do you avoid that?"

Pro: "By staying small, steady, and systematic. The Pro never bets survival on a single trade."

Pro: "The equation is simple: smaller risk per trade = lower risk of ruin."

"A good proven rule for Position Size is the foundation of a strong system."

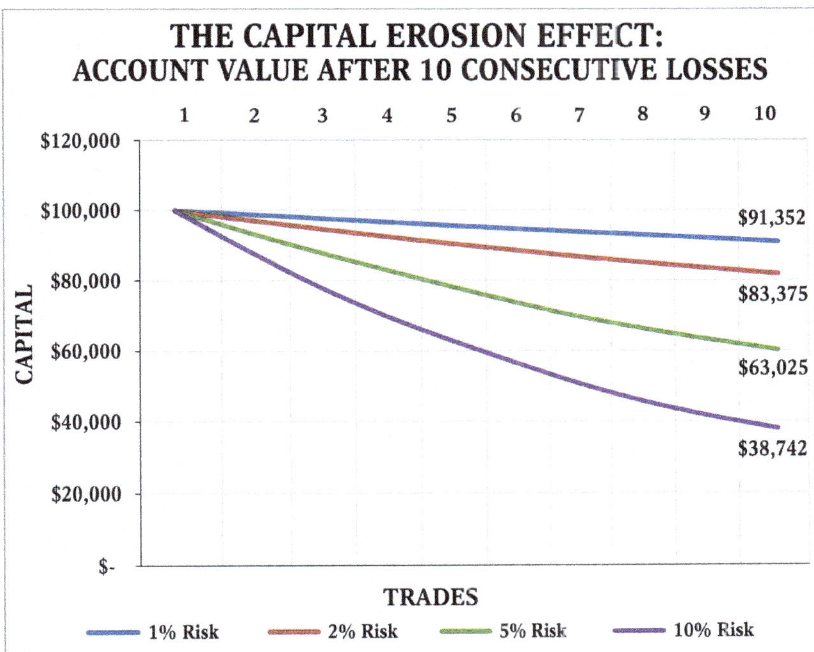

The Psychological Math

Pro: "Mathematical discipline builds psychological freedom. Once you know exactly what you can lose, fear disappears. The difference between gambling and trading is intent. Gamblers play for excitement; traders play for expectancy."

Particular	Gambler	Trader
Focus	Immediate Gratification	Long-Term Profitability
Risk	Undefined / All-in	Defined / Controlled (Fixed %)
Outcome	Hope / Luck	Probability / Statistical Edge
Decision Making	Intuition / Gut Feel	Systematic / Data-Driven
Mindset	Fear & Greed / Desperation	Discipline & Patience / Calm
Goal	Beat the Odds This Time	Let the Edge Play Out (Over Many Trades)
Position Sizing	Inconsistent / Too Large	Consistent / Appropriate
Longevity	Short-Term / Account Ruin Likely	Long-Term / Capital Preservation
Psychology	Volatile / Stressful	Stable / Freeing

The 1% Rule

Pro: "You'll hear me say this often, risk just 1% per trade until consistency proves otherwise. It may feel slow, but it keeps you alive long enough for your edge to compound.

Remember, a complete wipeout only happens if you lose 100 trades in a row and that's statistically improbable under tested edge."

Amateur: "But 1% feels small. It'll never grow."

Pro: "You're not growing an account, you're growing **competence**. Money follows mastery.

Create good profit buffers. Master yourself and then you're allowed to risk more."

"The Pro's wealth comes from staying in the game long enough for math to work."

Thinking Like a Business

Pro: "A business doesn't measure success daily. It measures quarterly, yearly, over hundreds of transactions. Trading is no different."

"Once you start thinking of trades as **transactions**, not emotional events, you become your own CFO."

Transactions, Not Emotions: Manage Your Financial Ledger
A Business Measures Success Over Many Transactions, Not Daily Swings.
OVERVIEW:
100 TRADE CYCLE
REVENUE (Your Winning Trades)
Trade 1: +$200
Trade 2: +$150
Expected Win Rate: 60%
+$150
+$250
Many More...
Many More...
EXPENSES (Your Losing Trades)
Trade A: -$50
Trade B: -$120
Expected Loss Rate: 40%
-$50
-$120
Many More...
Many More...
NET PROFIT / LOSS (Your Overall Expectancy)
REVENUE - EXPENSES = NET PROFIT
(60 x Avg Win) - (40 x Avg Loss) = $12,000 - $8,000 Net Profit
POSITIVE EXPECTANCY!
YOU'RE YOUR OWN CFO!
Think Like a CFO: Manage Revenue, Control Expenses, Focus on Long-Term Profitability

Final Reflection

Amateur: "So math isn't about making me rich, it's about keeping me sane."
Pro: "Exactly. Math is discipline disguised as numbers."

Chapter Summary

- Probability is random short-term, reliable long-term.
- Four Quadrants expanded: eliminate big losses, protect small wins.
- Expectancy formula defines profitability.
- 1% risk rule ensures survival.
- Avoid compounding drawdown.
- The lower the risk per trade, the lower the chance of ruin.
- Math is your emotional insurance.
- Treat trading like a business, consistent inputs create predictable outputs.

2.3 THE THIRD PILLAR, PSYCHOLOGICAL EDGE

You Don't Trade the Market, You Trade Yourself

Opening Scene

Amateur: "Pro, I've learned risk management, expectancy, position sizing…
Yet every time I'm in a trade, I panic. I know what to do, I just can't do it."

Pro: "That's because trading isn't a test of skill, it's a test of state.
The chart doesn't challenge your knowledge. It challenges your calm."

Why Psychology Is the Final Frontier

Pro: "You can learn systems from others, but you must build your psychology yourself.

In every field, sports, business, combat, performance is 90% mental.

Trading is no different. The math gives you direction, but mindset determines duration."

Psychology Is The Final Frontier

The Red Car Theory

Pro: "Ever heard of the Red Car Theory?"

Amateur: "The one where if you think of a red car, you suddenly see red cars everywhere?"

Pro: "Exactly.
In trading, the same thing happens. If you believe the market is 'against you,' you'll see traps everywhere. If you believe you're 'due a win,' you'll see opportunities that aren't there."

Pro: "What you focus on, multiplies."

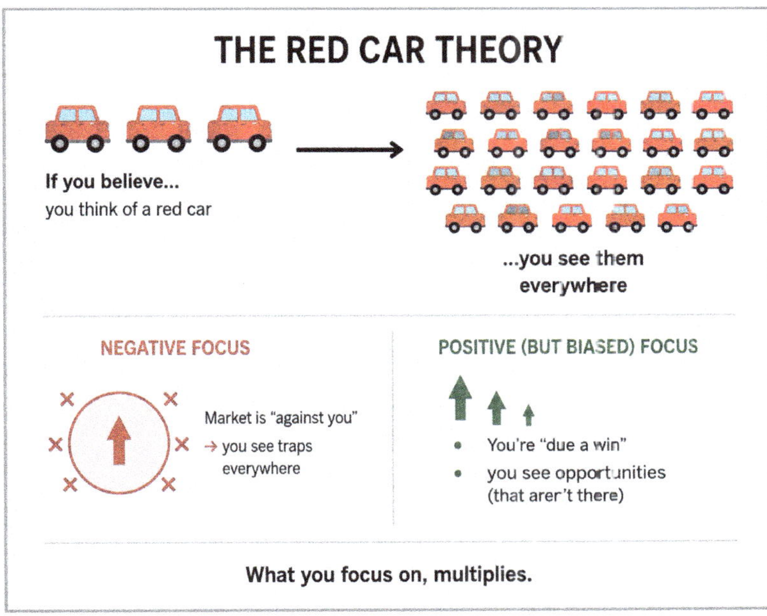

The 4 Trade Outcomes

Pro: "Every trade in your career will fall into one of four outcomes."

Outcome	Effect	Control
Big Win	Accelerates growth	Partial
Small Win	Feeds confidence	High
Small Loss	Tuition fee	High
Big Loss	Destroys account	Full prevention possible

Pro: "Notice something, the best traders simply remove the last box. They allow every other outcome, but they never let a small loss turn into a big one."

Amateur: "So even losing can be right, if it's controlled?"
Pro: "Exactly. Small losses are data; big losses are decisions."

The Trader's Emotional Cycle

Pro: "Let me show you what happens to most traders emotionally."

Stage	Feeling	Behaviour
Excitement	"This is the one!"	Over-leverage
Doubt	"Why isn't it moving?"	Exit too early
Fear	"It's reversing!"	Exit at loss
Regret	"It went my way after all…"	Revenge trade

Pro: "They repeat this loop endlessly until they burn out."

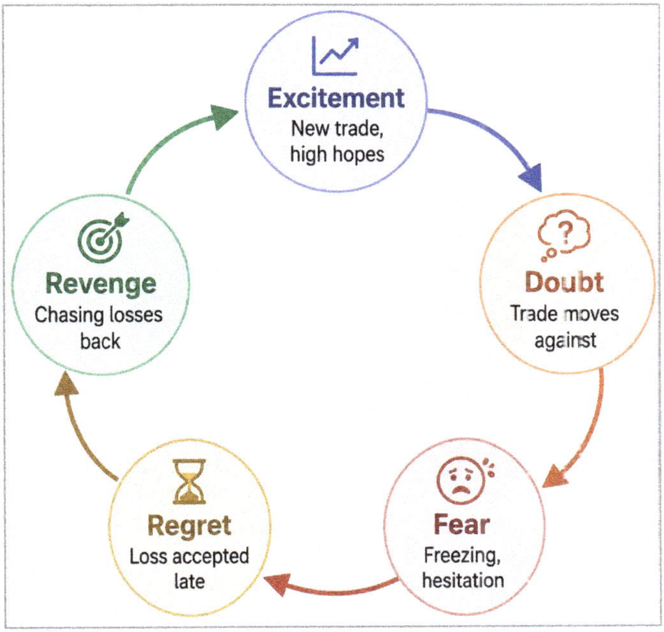

Pro: "The professional breaks the loop by separating identity from outcome.
You are not your last trade."

The Gambler vs The Professional

Pro: "Want to know the real difference between a gambler and a professional?"

Aspect	Gambler	Professional Trader
Goal	Excitement	Longevity
Approach	Random risk	Fixed risk
Reaction	Hope	Adaptation
Time Frame	Short	Infinite
Focus	Money	Process

Pro: "Gambler's trade to feel alive.
Professionals trade so their system can live."

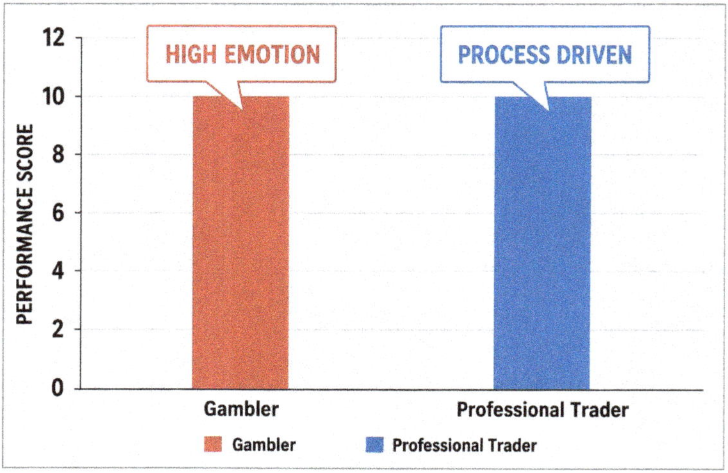

Amateur: "So the gambler needs the thrill; the pro needs the calm."
Pro: "Exactly. The gambler chases dopamine; the pro builds discipline."

Acceptance: The Hardest Skill

Pro: "Acceptance doesn't mean you enjoy losing. It means you don't resist reality. If you can't accept being wrong, you'll never let your winners run, because you'll always need to be right."

Amateur: "So accepting loss actually protects profit?"
Pro: "Yes. Paradoxical, isn't it?"

"You can't hold profits without learning to accept losses."

The Mind-Body Connection

Pro: "Your state of mind changes how you trade. When your breathing is fast, your timeframes shrink. When you're calm, your perspective expands."

"That's why pros have rituals, breathing, meditation, journaling. It's not superstition; it's state management."

Pro: "If your body is chaotic, your entries will be too."

Journaling: The Mirror That Speaks

Pro: "The fastest way to grow in trading? Journal honestly."

He opened a worn notebook.

Pro: "This isn't a diary of profit. It's a record of behaviour especially the emotions before, after & during the trade. Write what you felt, not just what you earned."

Example Entry	Emotion	Lesson
Exited early	Fear	Trust process next time
Added too soon	Greed	Follow plan, not impulse
Followed plan perfectly	Calm	Reinforce this habit

Pro: "Your journal is a mirror. It tells you what your P&L can't."

Key things to include in Journal (Do these for all trades, review & improvise)

Category	Field	Description
Trade Details	**Instrument**	Name of the asset traded (e.g., NAS100, Gold, NIFTY)
	Buy / Sell	Direction of trade
	Quantity	Number of units or lot size
	Stop-Loss (SL)	Level of risk protection
	Risk %	Percentage of capital risked
	Planned Target	Expected exit point
	Actual Exit	Final closed level
	Planned R:R	Expected Risk-to-Reward ratio
	Actual R:R	Actual Risk-to-Reward achieved
	Profit %	Gain or loss percentage
Trade Psychology	**Aspect**	Reflection
	Entry Reason	Why you took the trade (setup, confluence, bias)
	Exit Reason	What triggered your exit
	Mistakes	Any deviation from the plan
	Lessons Learned	Key insights to improve future trades
	Did I Follow My Rules?	✅ Yes / ❌ No
	Stage	What You Felt
Emotional Journal	**Before Trade**	(e.g., confident, doubtful, anxious)
	During Trade	(e.g., excited, fearful, impulsive)
	After Trade	(e.g., relieved, proud, frustrated)

The Power of Pause

Pro: "Professionals know when not to trade. Stillness is part of their edge."

"When emotions rise, step away.

Walk, breathe, detach. You don't lose by not trading, you lose by forcing."

Amateur: "So discipline isn't only about doing. It's also about not doing."
Pro: "Exactly."

"Discipline is choosing patience over participation."

The Shift from Emotion to Execution

Pro: "Here's the final stage, when you stop asking, 'Did I win?' and start asking, 'Did I execute as per the system?'"

"That's when you've built your psychological edge. The market still moves the same way, but you don't."

"The Professionals too feel emotion, but doesn't act on it.
The Amateur acts first, and then feels."

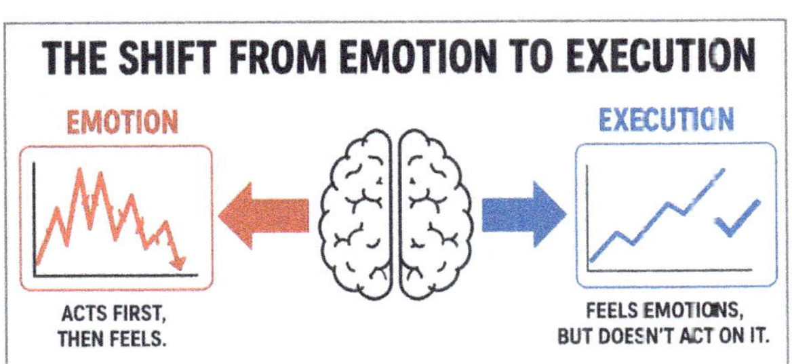

Final Reflection

Amateur: "So trading isn't about fighting fear. It's about coexisting with it."

Pro: "Exactly. Fear never leaves; it just learns its place."

Chapter Summary

- Psychology is 90% of consistent performance.
- Red Car Theory: you see what you believe.
- Four Trade Outcomes: eliminate big losses, accept small ones.
- Gamblers seek thrill; professionals seek peace.
- Acceptance is the bridge between chaos and control.
- Journaling reveals truth data can't.
- Stillness is a position too.
- Execution matters more than emotion.

PART 3: THE MARKET'S REALITY

"The market doesn't deceive you; your expectations do."

3.1 MYTHS THAT DESTROY TRADERS

"The Stories We Tell Ourselves to Feel Safe"

Opening Scene

Amateur: "Pro, I think I'm cursed. Every time I find a good setup, it fails.
Maybe indicators just don't work?"

Pro: "Indicators work fine. The question is, do you work with them properly?"

The "Indicator Failed" Myth

Pro: "Indicators never fail, expectations do. They summarize price action; they don't predict the future."

"Most traders use them as fortune tellers instead of thermometers."

Myth	Reality
RSI tells me when to buy	RSI shows relative momentum
EMA crossover = new trend	It confirms what already started
Volume spike = reversal	It only shows participation, not direction

Pro: "You can't blame the tool when you use it like a magic wand."

The "Market Hunts My Stops" Myth

Pro: "The market doesn't know you exist. It moves to where liquidity sits."

He drew a quick sketch.

"Below visible lows and above obvious highs sit clusters of stop orders.

That's free liquidity. The market clears those levels to fill big orders."

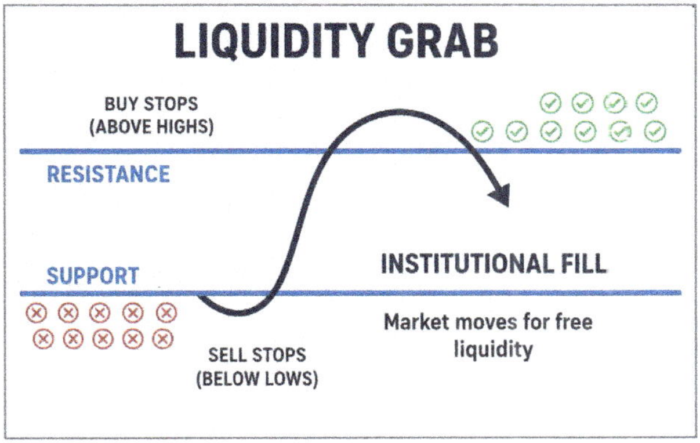

Amateur: "So it's not personal, it's plumbing."
Pro: "Exactly."

The "I Need a Higher Win Rate" Myth

Pro: "Amateurs worship accuracy; professionals worship expectancy.

Profit = (Win % × Average Win) – (Loss % × Average Loss)

"You can be right 40% of the time and still make money if your winners are twice your losers."

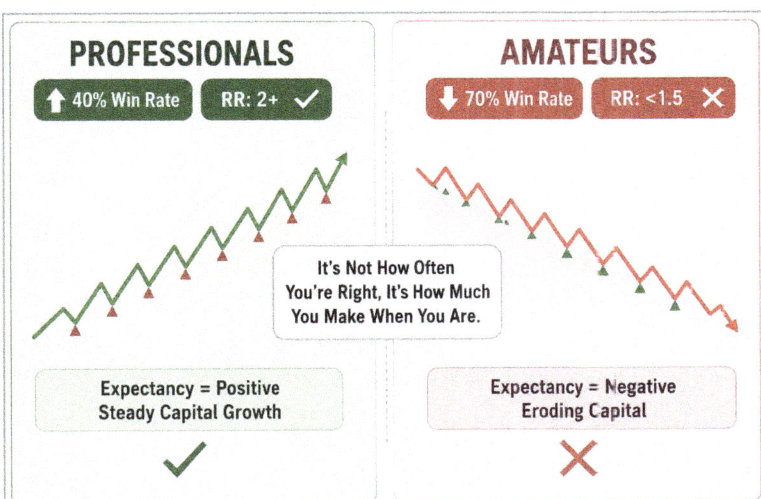

The Cost of One Emotional Trade

Pro: "There was a day I hit my daily loss limit. I knew the rule: stop trading. But I told myself: just one clean setup to recover. That one trade erased a week of disciplined work.

Revenge trading doesn't destroy accounts in one blow. It destroys trust in yourself."

The "Perfect Timing" Myth

Amateur: "But Pro, I saw a trader say he caught the full move, from the exact bottom to the exact top!"
Pro: "Then you've met either God, or a liar. Once in a while, luck lines up, maybe they caught one perfect entry and exit. But if they claim to do it often, they're selling fantasy, not truth. Thousands of participants are buying and selling at the same time. No one can consistently predict **where every buyer will stop or every seller will start.** The market is too complex, too fluid and beautifully unpredictable."

"If someone says they catch every move, they're either God or a liar.
It's you who must decide."

"The goal isn't to catch the entire move; it's to capture the part that belongs to your plan and protect it."

The "Big Move Means Big Opportunity" Myth

Pro: "Volatility is noise in costume. The same candle that excites you terrifies someone else."

Situation	Amateur's Reaction	Pro's Action
Sudden Breakout	Enters Impulsively	Waits For Retest
Sharp Drop	Panics & Exits	Watches Liquidity Levels

Pro: "A big move doesn't mean opportunity, it means emotion."

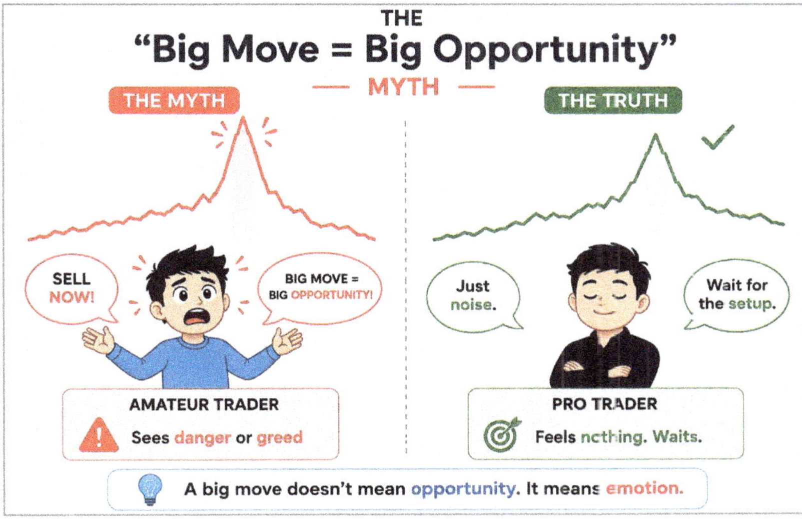

The "If I Learn More, I'll Earn More" Myth

Pro: "More information often means more confusion. Knowledge helps only when filtered through experience. The aim is NOT to take PhD in trading or market knowledge; goal is to make consistent income from trading. Don't collect systems. Master one lens and polish it."

"The moment you stop blaming the market, learning begins."

Final Reflection

Amateur: "So it's not about perfect tools, it's about perfect discipline."

Pro: "Exactly. Tools measure the market. Discipline measures you."

Chapter Summary

- Indicators describe, not predict.
- Liquidity hunts orders, not individuals.
- Expectancy > Accuracy.
- No one times every move. The goal is to capture what's yours and protect it.
- Volatility equals emotion.
- Mastery comes from depth, not data.

3.2 THE MARKET WILL DECEIVE YOU

Understanding Traps, Cycles, and the Psychology of Volatility

---

Opening Scene

Amateur: "I did everything right: confirmation, entry, stop, and it still reversed.

The market tricked me again."

Pro: "The market didn't trick you. It just told a story you wanted to believe."

The Cycle of Deception

Pro: "Every major move begins with emotional imbalance."

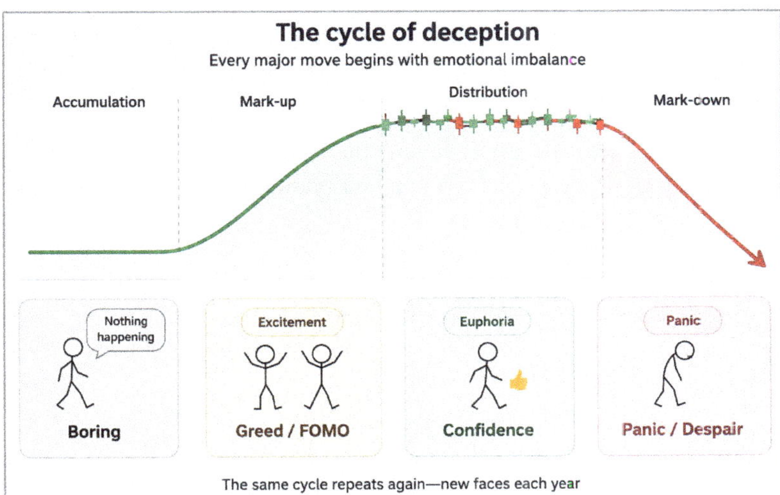

Pro: "It's the same cycle repeating with new faces each year."

Trend vs Counter-Trend

Pro: "Most traders lose because they fight structure. They call every pullback a reversal."

Trader Type	Belief	Result
Trend Follower	"It'll continue."	Rides the wave
Counter-Trend trader	"It's overextended."	Fights momentum

Pro: "Neither is wrong, until ego joins the trade.

The key is alignment, not prediction."

Predicting the Market Is Impossible

Amateur: "So, is there any way to really time the market?"

Pro: "If you could, you'd be the first human in history to do so. Think about it, you can't even predict what ten people at a dinner table will say next. You don't know what the person sitting beside you will order, what the next one will laugh at, or when someone will interrupt.

Now imagine trying to predict what millions of independent traders, investors, and algorithms around the world will do, all at once, with different goals, emotions, and timeframes.

That's what trying to 'perfectly time the market' really means. So, when someone says they catch every top and bottom. They're either God, or they're lying."

"Once in a while, luck aligns, but never consistently.

The goal isn't perfection; it's participation with control."

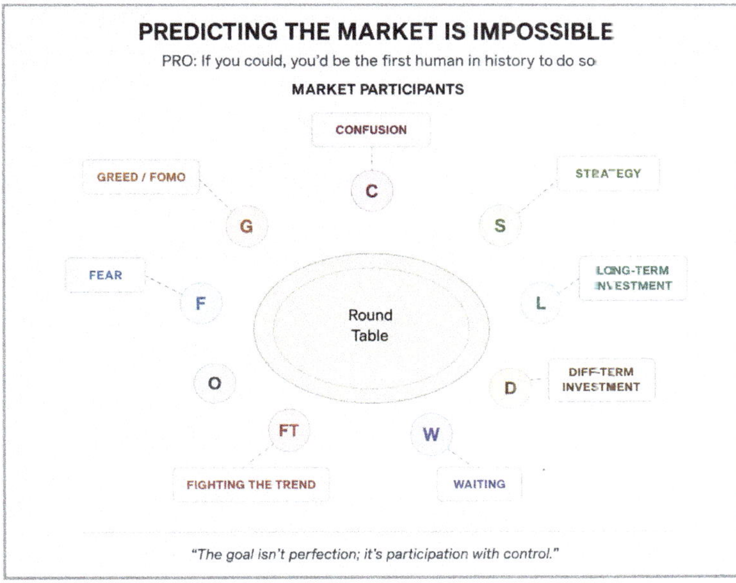

How Liquidity Creates Traps

Pro: "Before big moves, the market needs orders, and trapped traders provide them. Breakouts above highs lure buyers; price then reverses to collect liquidity."

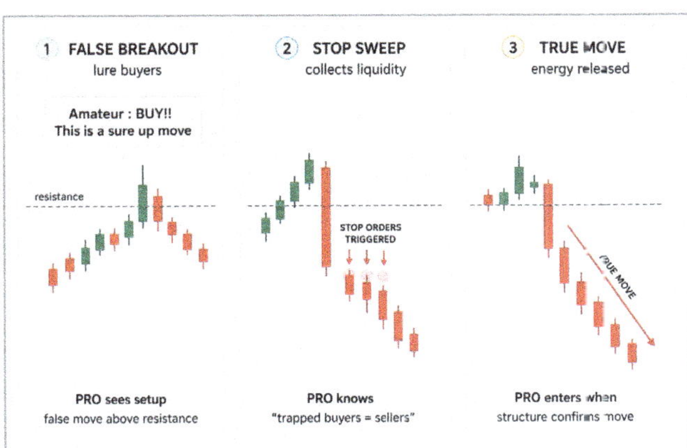

Amateur: "So fakeouts are part of the process?"

Pro: "Exactly. Traps aren't accidents, they're fuel. When the real move begins, most retail traders are already trapped in losses. Their confidence fades, their capital shrinks, and their mind hesitates when the true opportunity finally appears. That's how the market balances itself, by transferring energy from impatience to patience."

"Liquidity traps don't hunt traders, they hunt impatience"

Why You See Patterns That Aren't There

Pro: "Your brain is a pattern-making machine. In randomness, it creates stories, comfort in chaos. Professionals see possibilities; Amateurs see promises."

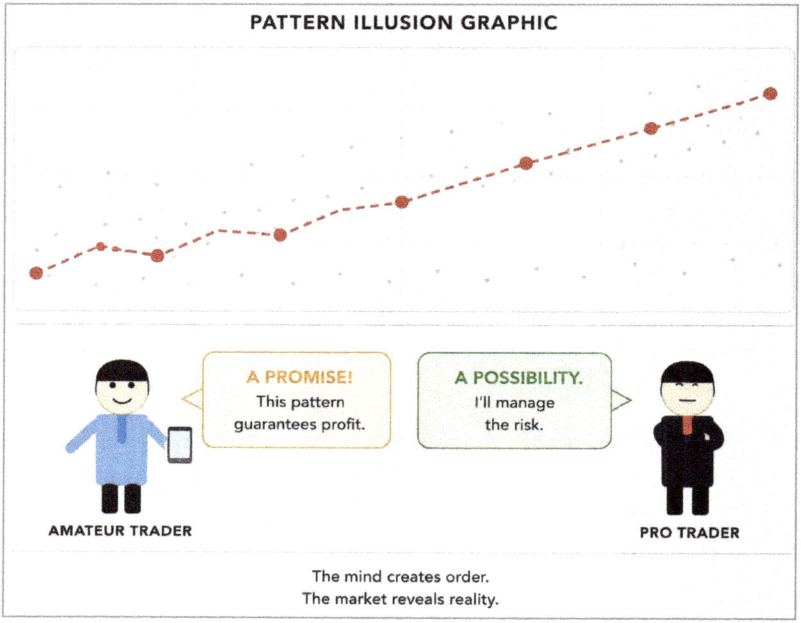

Managing Uncertainty

Pro: "Since deception is unavoidable, management is your only defence."

Principle	Application
Wait for confirmation	Delay impulse
Risk small	Buy survival
Journal deception	Recognize repetition
Accept traps	Stop personalizing losses

Pro: "The Pro isn't surprised by traps, he anticipates them."

Volatility and Emotion

Pro: "Volatility feels exciting because it mirrors emotion. Calm charts bore you because they reflect stability."

"Train yourself to find peace in boredom, that's where real trades build."

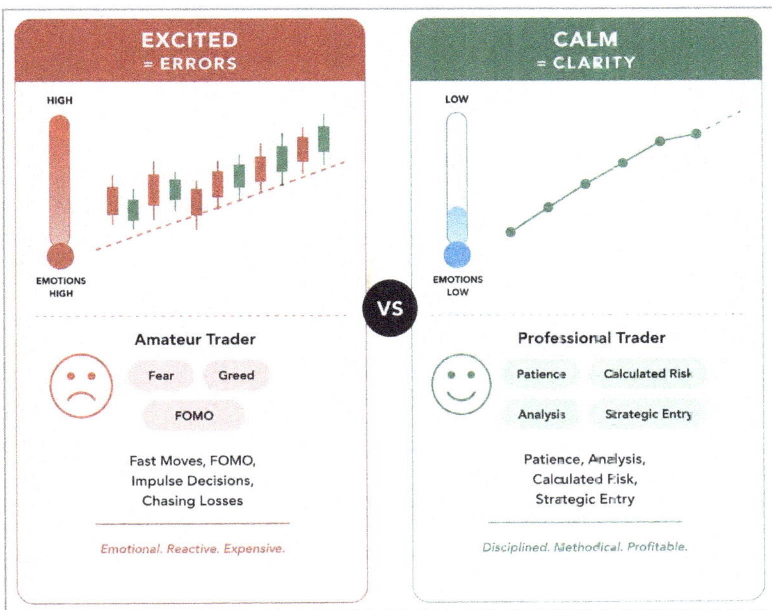

The Shift from Victim to Observer

Pro: "Stop thinking 'the market did this to me.' Start thinking 'I reacted this way to the market.'

That one shift turns pain into perspective."

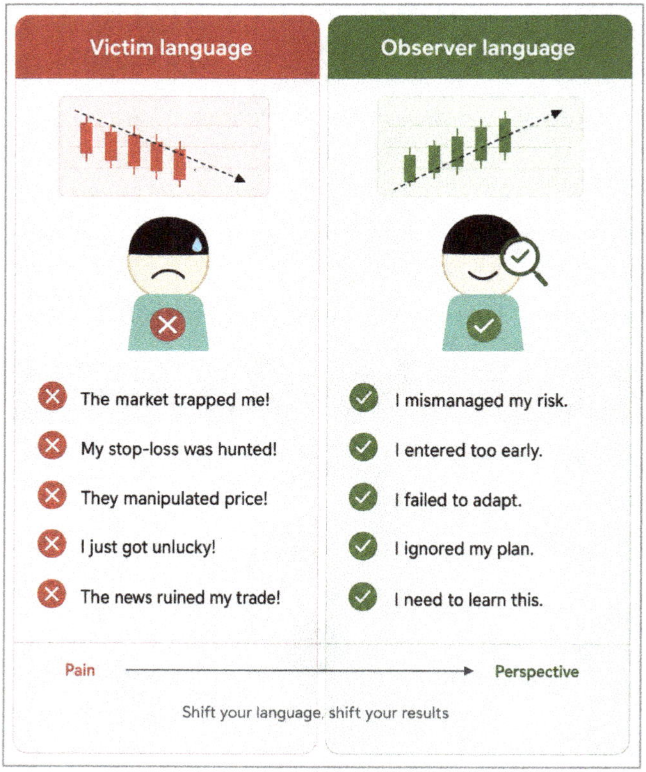

"The market's deception isn't personal, it's structural."

Final Reflection

Amateur: "So fakeouts, volatility, and traps, they're all just part of the ecosystem."

Pro: "Exactly.
The sooner you stop fighting them, the sooner you'll flow with them."

Chapter Summary

• Market cycles repeat through human emotion.
• Trend vs counter-trend is about alignment, not ego.
• Perfectly timing the market is impossible, you can only react wisely, not predict perfectly.
• Liquidity creates traps; traps create opportunity.
• Pattern-seeking is psychological comfort.
• Accept randomness, manage exposure, observe objectively.

3.3 THE INVISIBLE ENEMY

"Cognitive Biases That Quietly Destroy Traders"

Opening Scene

Amateur: "Pro, sometimes I know the rule… but I still break it. It feels like something inside me pushes me."

Pro nodded calmly. "That 'something' has a name. **Bias**."

"You are not fighting the market. You are fighting your brain."

"Every trader believes the market is the opponent. Very few realize the real opponent sits behind the eyes."

What Is a Cognitive Bias?

Pro: "A cognitive bias is a mental shortcut. Your brain uses it to save energy. In daily life, shortcuts help. In trading, they distort judgment. The market is neutral. The brain is not."

<u>1. Loss Aversion: Why Losing Hurts More Than Winning Feels Good</u>

Pro: "Loss aversion means you feel losses roughly twice as strongly as gains. That's why traders:

- Move stop-loss further
- Average into losing positions
- Refuse to exit
- Close winners too early"

Amateur: "Because I don't want to feel the pain."

Pro: "Exactly. You're not managing risk. You're managing emotion."

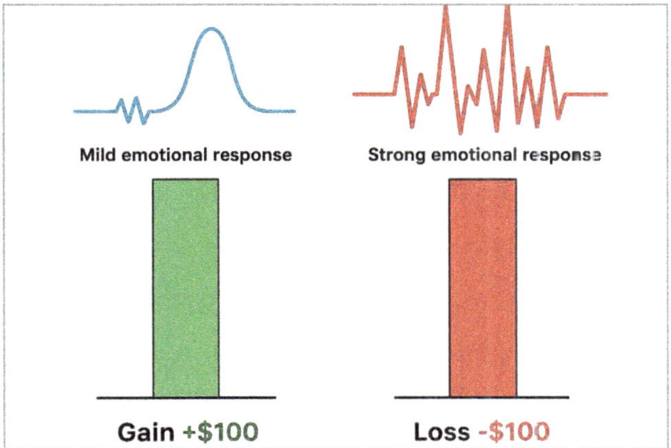

2. Confirmation Bias: Why You See Only What You Want to See

Pro: "Once you enter a trade, your brain looks for evidence that supports your decision. You ignore invalidation. You search for agreement."

Amateur: "So I don't want truth. I want comfort."

Pro: "Yes. Confirmation bias turns analysis into defence. You stop evaluating the chart. You start protecting your ego."

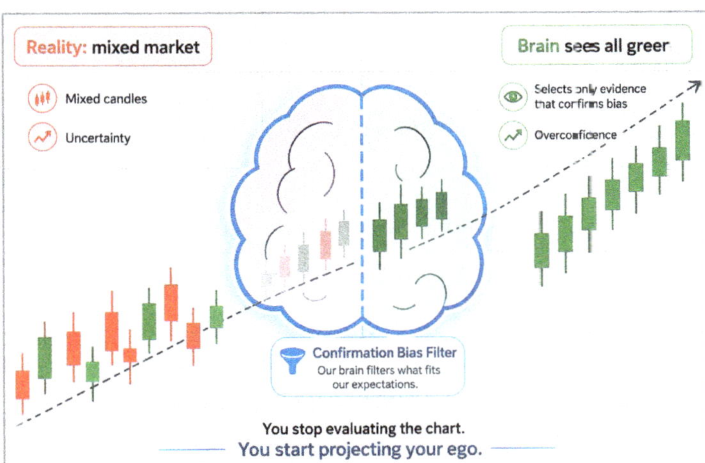

3. Recency Bias: Why the Last Few Trades Control You

Pro: "If you win three trades, you feel invincible. If you lose three, you feel broken. That's recency bias. You shrink your sample size from 100 trades to 3."

Amateur: "So I react to streaks instead of probabilities."

Pro: "Exactly. Professionals think in series. Amateurs think in streaks."

4. Overconfidence Bias: The Silent Killer After Success

Pro: "Overconfidence rarely appears at the beginning. It appears after success. You increase size too quickly. Skip confirmations. Break risk rules."

Amateur: "Because I think I've figured it out."

Pro: "The market punishes certainty. Confidence without structure becomes destruction."

Confidence trades emotion. Conviction trades data.

---

5. The Sunk Cost Fallacy: Why You Stay in Losing Trades

Pro: "If you've already lost 3%, your brain says, Let me wait. I've invested too much to exit now. That's sunk cost bias. You're not protecting capital. You're protecting pride."

Amateur: "So I stay longer because I've already stayed too long."

Pro: "And that logic destroys accounts."

6. Authority Bias: Why You Blindly Trust Gurus

Pro: "When someone speaks confidently, shows luxury, or uses complex language, your brain assigns authority. You stop questioning. That's why fake mentors succeed. Authority bias replaces scepticism with admiration."

7. Availability Bias: Why Dramatic Moves Feel Common

Pro: "You remember breakouts and crashes vividly. You forget slow consolidation. So, you chase volatility. Your brain remembers drama more than stability."

The Core Insight

Amateur: "So I'm not irrational… I'm wired this way?"

Pro: "Yes. Bias is biological. Unmanaged bias is destructive The goal isn't to eliminate bias. It's to design systems that neutralize it."

How Professionals Contain Bias

Pro wrote down five structural protections:

1. Predefine entry and exit before execution
2. Fix risk per trade
3. Journal decisions immediately
4. Review weekly, not emotionally
5. Think in 100-trade samples

"Bias weakens when structure strengthens."

Consolidated Bias Map

Bias	Amateur Reaction	Professional Response
Loss Aversion Bias	Moves stop-loss	Accepts predefined risk
Confirmation Bias	Seeks agreement	Seeks invalidation
Recency Bias	Reacts to streak	Thinks in large samples
Overconfidence Bias	Increases size	Increases patience
Sunk Cost Fallacy	Holds losing trade	Exits by rule

Authority Bias	Blind trust	Independent verification
Availability Bias	Chases volatility	Waits for structure

Final Reflection

Amateur: "So discipline is bias control."

Pro: "Exactly. Trading is not intelligence superiority. It is bias management superiority. The market doesn't defeat traders. Their unexamined thinking does."

Chapter Summary

- Loss aversion distorts exits.
- Confirmation bias blinds objectivity.
- Recency bias shrinks sample size.
- Overconfidence follows success.
- Sunk cost traps capital.
- Authority bias enables illusion.
- Availability bias fuels impulsive trades.
- Structure reduces psychological distortion.

PART 4: PATH TO PROFITABILITY

*"You don't rise by trading more.
You rise by repeating what works, quietly."*

4.1 FROM AMATEUR TO CONSISTENT

"Consistency > Accuracy"

Opening Scene

Amateur: "Pro, I think I'm improving, my losses don't hurt as much, and I don't chase every candle. But I still can't call myself consistent."

Pro: "Consistency isn't a feeling. It's a pattern. And patterns appear only through repetition."

What Consistency Actually Means

Pro: "Most traders define consistency as winning often. Professionals define it as behaving identically."

Amateur's Definition	
Same result every day	Same process every trade
Excitement from profits	Calm from discipline
Measures by money	Measures by execution

The Cycle of Consistency

Pro: "Every Pro lives inside one simple loop."

Pro: "Repetition isn't boring, it's reinforcement."

The 100-Trade Challenge

Pro: "Here's your next assignment, the 100-Trade Challenge."

Amateur: "100 trades? That's a lot!"

Pro: "It's not about number, it's about data. After 100 executed trades with identical risk, your real edge will reveal itself."

Rules:

- ☐ Risk 1% per trade.
- ☐ Journal every trade (entry, exit, emotion).
- ☐ Make no strategy changes mid-challenge.
- ☐ Review only after 100 trades, not before.

Pro: "This is how you separate randomness from reality."

Building Your Feedback System

Pro: "Without feedback, improvement is guesswork." He opened his journal.

Metric	Purpose	Explanation
Win %	**Gauge probability distribution**	This metric tracks how often the strategy results in a win. It helps a trader understand the statistical likelihood of success for their chosen setups over time.
Average R:R (Average Risk: Reward)	**Ensure positive expectancy**	This is the most crucial metric. It calculates the average profit (in relation to risk taken) versus the average loss. A strategy with a Win % below 50% can still be highly profitable if the Average R:R is high enough (e.g., $2 profit for every $1 risked). **Positive expectancy** is the mathematical foundation of long-term profitability.
Emotional Score (1–5)	**Track state vs outcome**	This is a psychological metric. By rating their emotional state (e.g., 1=Calm, 5=Panicked) before, during, or after a trade, the trader can identify how specific emotions (greed, fear) correlate with positive or negative outcomes.
Mistake Tag	**Identify repeat errors**	This involves tagging trades with categories like "Impulsive Entry," "Moved Stop-Loss," or "Missed Setup." It quickly highlights the **most common behavioural flaws** that need correction, turning abstract frustration into concrete, addressable issues.

Pro: "You don't need a mentor forever, you need mirrors."

The Discipline Triangle

Pro: "Consistency rests on three sides, Process, Discipline, Reflection."

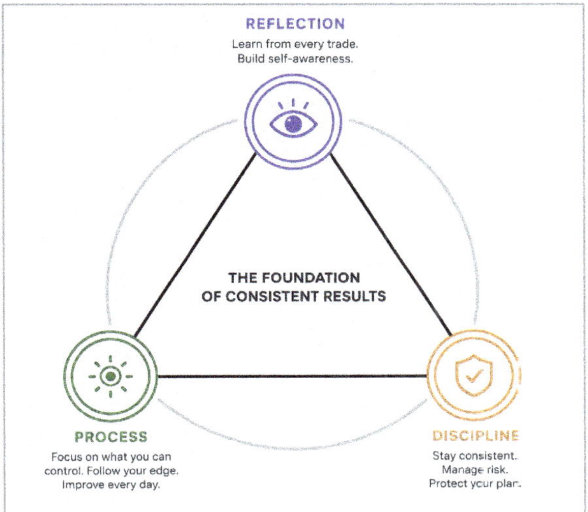

"Process keeps you organized. Discipline keeps you obedient. Reflection keeps you evolving."

Turning Losses into Lessons

Pro: "Every loss gives feedback. Record what triggered it: fear, greed, over-confidence, boredom."

Trigger	Correction
Fear	Smaller size, breathe
Greed	Pre-define targets
Boredom	Step away
Over-confidence	Pause after big win

Pro: "You can't fix what you refuse to see."

Routines Create Results

Pro: "Your day defines your data."

Time Block	Focus
Pre-Market	Meditation, Plan Checklist
Trading Hours	Execute only pre-approved setups
Post-Market	Journal & Review
Off-Hours	Study & back-test, not profits

Pro: "Small habits stack into stability."

"Consistency arrives when discipline replaces dopamine."

Final Reflection

Amateur: "So I don't need new strategies, I need new habits."
Pro: "Exactly. Systems don't fail, discipline does."

Chapter Summary

- Consistency = repetition + reflection.
- Follow the Cycle of Consistency.
- 100-Trade Challenge reveals your true edge.
- Journaling turns mistakes into metrics.
- Routines create results.
- Dopamine dies where discipline begins.

4.2 THE EQUITY CURVE REALITY

"The Journey of Growth Through Drawdowns"

Opening Scene

Amateur: "Pro, I've been journaling every trade and following my plan, but my account still goes up and down. Shouldn't consistency make my curve smoother?"

Pro: "Consistency makes your behaviour stable, not your curve. The market still breathes; your equity line will too."

The Myth of a Straight Line

Pro: "Traders want their equity curve to rise like a staircase, step after step, clean and predictable. But real equity curves look like mountains, peaks of wins, valleys of drawdowns, and long flat plains of boredom. A smooth curve is a fantasy. A rising but uneven curve is mastery."

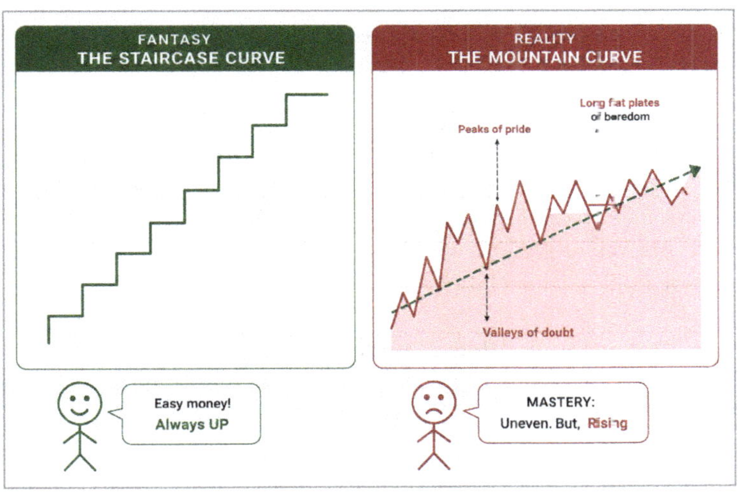

Why Drawdowns Are Natural

Pro: "Every edge works in streaks, clusters of wins and losses. You might have four losses in a row, then five wins that more than cover them. That's probability, not punishment. A trader who panics during a drawdown kills his own edge, because the recovery that follows never gets a chance."

Example: The $100,000 Journey

Pro: "Let's take an example. You start with $100,000, risking 1% per trade."

Scenario	Result
Win 2 trades, lose 3	Equity: $99,000
Next 5 wins in a row	Equity: $104,000
Two more losses	Equity: $102,000
Three strong wins	Equity: $107,000

"This is normal. You're still growing, just not in a straight line. Judge your progress every 50–100 trades, not every week. Zoom out, clarity lives in distance."

The Danger of Forcing Growth

Pro: "Traders destroy their curves when they try to accelerate them. If your system's natural expectancy gives 2–3% monthly, forcing 10% won't speed up growth, it'll speed up ruin. The goal isn't to make money every week; it's to avoid losing yourself every week."

How Professionals View Equity

Amateur's View	Pro's View
"I lost money this week."	"I'm inside expected variance."
"My curve dipped, I failed."	"My edge is playing out long-term."
"I need to win back losses."	"I need to follow process."

Pro: "Professionals see drawdowns as data, not as disaster."

The Emotional Slope

Pro: "The equity curve isn't just a line on your account; it's a mirror of your emotion."

"When the line dips, your belief is tested. When it rises, your humility is tested."

"Handle both with discipline, and the slope stays upward."

"A smooth curve is a lie; a rising curve through drawdowns is the truth."

Final Reflection

Amateur: "So the goal isn't to make it smooth; it's to make it rise despite the dips."
Pro: "Exactly. The market doesn't reward the trader who avoids drawdowns, it rewards the one who survives them."

Chapter Summary

- Real equity growth is uneven and unpredictable.
- Drawdowns are part of probability, not punishment.
- Zoom out; evaluate every 100 trades, not 10.
- Forcing returns breaks edges.
- Professionals view drawdowns as data.
- Survival keeps the slope upward.

4.3 THE TRADER'S EVOLUTION

"Growth is invisible in the moment, until one day, patience looks like power."

Opening Scene

The Amateur had been trading consistently for six months. He wasn't making millions, but he wasn't losing anymore either. His charts were cleaner, his journal thicker, and his emotions quieter. He looked at the Pro, a calm smile on his face.

Amateur: "Pro, I finally feel stable. My results are steady, and my mindset feels balanced. But now I want to take the next step; I want to increase my size. Is that the right time?"

The Pro looked up slowly, smiled, and said,

Pro: "It's the right time to evolve, but evolution has its own risks."

The Natural Phases of a Trader

Pro: "Every trader passes through four inevitable stages."

He wrote them on the whiteboard:

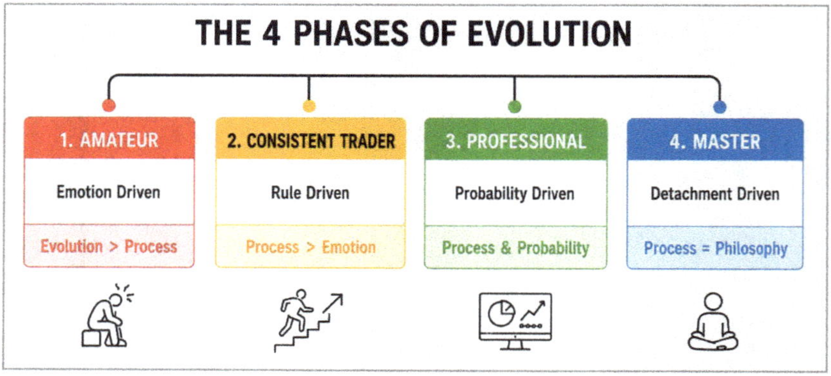

You evolve not by finding new markets, but mastering yourself in every market

Pro: "You start by reacting to the market. Then you learn to respond. Eventually, you realize you don't react at all, you just execute."

Amateur smiled. "So, the next level isn't about a new setup, it's about a new self."

Pro: "Exactly. Growth in trading isn't vertical. It's internal."

When Size Grew Faster Than Stability

Pro: "There was a month I performed beautifully. Clean execution. Strong returns. So, I increased size the next month. The math stayed the same. The emotion didn't. One impulsive deviation cost me the entire previous month's gain. That's when I understood: You don't scale capital. You scale character."

The Pressure of Scaling

Pro: "Here's the irony. when you start winning consistently, your biggest enemy changes. It's no longer losing. It's expectation. He drew a chart with 2 line; one showing emotional spikes of a beginner, another flat line of a consistent trader. Then he added a sudden jump: Scaling Phase."

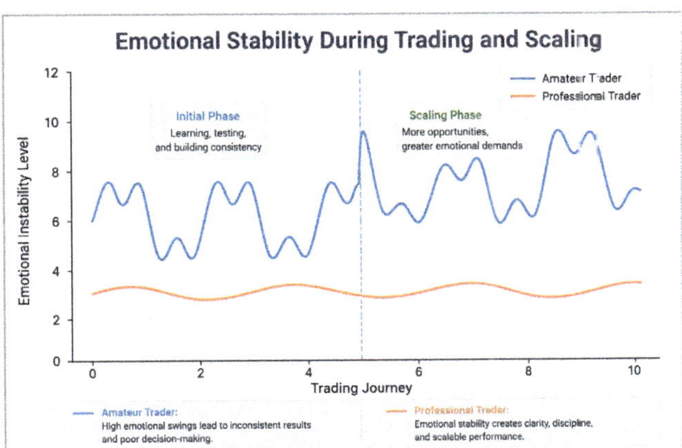

Pro: "When you scale up your capital, you also scale up your emotions. The same 1% loss now feels like a mountain, not because the system changed, but because the size did."

Amateur nodded slowly. "So, the numbers are the same, but the pressure isn't."

Pro: "Exactly. Scaling without emotional adaptation is the fastest way back to inconsistency."

"Your account grows faster than your psychology, unless you train both."

The Right Way to Scale

Pro: "Most traders make the mistake of doubling their size instantly when they see profits. That's gambling with a better disguise.

He listed the proper approach:

- Scale in percentages, not emotions. Increase position size only after a stable sample (e.g., 30 trades with positive expectancy).
- Recalculate risk per trade. Keep the same percentage (1–2%), even as the account grows.
- Recalibrate expectations. The goal is not to make more, it's to maintain stability at scale.

Pro: "You earn the right to size up, not because you made money, but because you proved you can stay calm. That's what separates a professional from a performer. Professionals don't increase size after a good week; they increase size after good control. You don't lift heavier weights by skipping warm-ups. You increase strength by progressive overload, same in trading."

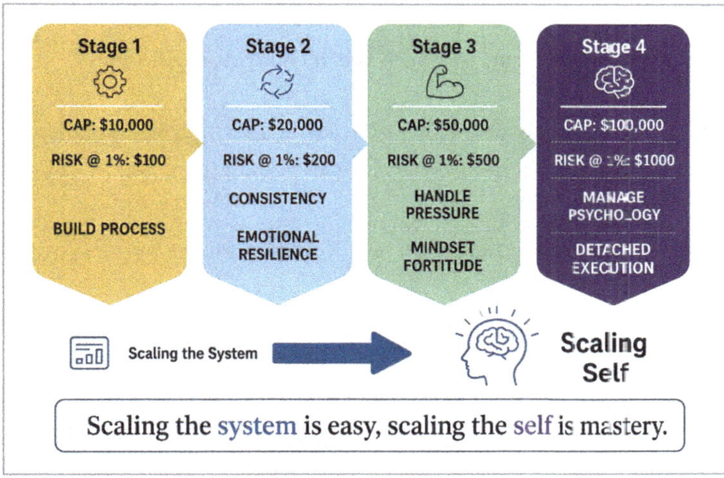

NOTE: Capital represented are for example purpose.

The Psychology of Growth

Pro: "When numbers get bigger, your brain starts to distort scale."

He continued, "You used to see $500 as a normal loss. Now, at higher capital, it's $5,000; same 1%, but it feels 10× worse."

Amateur exhaled. "So, my math didn't change, my mind did."

Pro: "Exactly. This is why the next level of evolution is mental conditioning, not market knowledge."

"Scaling tests what's left of your emotional weakness."

The Professional's Habits

Pro: "Professionals have habits that protect them from emotional interference."

He listed a few on the board:

- Fixed risk per trade: Never above pre-defined %

- Scheduled review: Weekly system performance check
- Drawdown limit: Step away when equity drops beyond threshold
- Rest and recovery: Treat losses like muscle fatigue, not failure
- Data tracking: Monthly performance audit (expectancy, win rate, risk ratio)

Pro: "They treat trading like a business. You can't grow a business by guessing. You grow it by measuring."

METRIC	PURPOSE
Win %	Check probability alignment.
Avg R:R Average Risk:Reward	Ensure expectancy remains positive.
Max Drawdown	Detect early emotional slippage.
Journal Notes	Capture recurring patterns.
Action Plan	Adjust for next week.

Pro: "Professionals don't react to outcomes; they refine their process."

"Scaling capital without scaling character is a setup for self-destruction."

The Ego Trap at Higher Levels

Pro: "The hardest test of evolution is ego; it comes disguised as confidence. When you start winning regularly, your ego whispers, you've outgrown the rules. It tells you to size up faster, skip confirmations, or take impulsive setups."

Amateur laughed softly. "That's exactly what I did last week, **it cost me an entire month's profit.**"

Pro: "That's how ego works. It doesn't shout; it negotiates."

"Ego doesn't appear at the start of your journey; it waits until you're good enough to believe you don't need rules."

The Shift from Confidence to Conviction

Pro: "Confidence is emotional, conviction is mathematical. Confidence says, I feel good about this trade. Conviction says, I have data that supports this trade."

Pro: "Professionals trade conviction. Amateurs trade confidence."

Pro: "when you replace confidence with conviction, you become unshakeable".

The True Definition of a Professional

Pro: "A professional trader isn't defined by account size; but by behaviour under stress."

He paused, letting that sink in.

"When you can follow your system after a losing streak… When you can trade small even when you're tempted to trade big…When you can walk away when your mind says "stay ", that's professionalism."

Amateur nodded quietly. "So being a pro isn't about how much I make, **it's about how little I deviate.**"

Pro: "Exactly. Freedom in trading comes from obedience, not rebellion."

"Professionals don't feel less fear; they just act less emotionally."

The Master Phase: Detachment

Pro: "There's one last stage, the Master. The Master doesn't trade for money. He trades for process. Wins and losses don't define his self-worth anymore. At this stage, trading becomes a reflection of who you are, not what you earn. When you no longer chase the market, the market follows your rhythm."

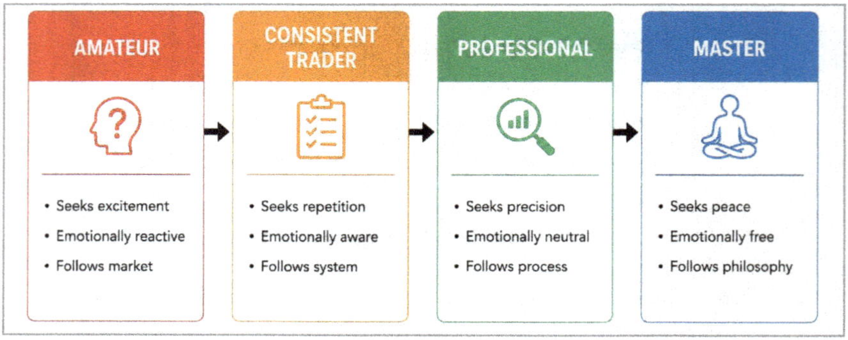

Closing Reflection

Pro: "Exactly. The real destination isn't financial freedom, it's emotional freedom."

He looked at the Amateur warmly. "And once you find that, you'll realize… the market was never your opponent. It was your teacher."

Amateur closed his journal slowly, a smile spreading across his face. "You know, Pro, I used to think evolution meant becoming fearless. But now I realize it means becoming peaceful."

Final Takeaway

The trader's evolution begins with emotion, matures with discipline, and ends with detachment.

Chapter Summary

- Evolution in trading is internal, not external.
- Scaling multiplies emotions, not just profits.
- Professionals focus on process, not performance.
- Ego grows with success; discipline must grow faster.
- True mastery is emotional detachment, not fearlessness.

4.4 TRADING STYLES: SPEED, STRENGTH & STABILITY

"Finding the Rhythm That Fits You"

Opening Scene

Amateur: "Pro, I think I'm finally consistent. I can follow my plan without panicking. But now I'm unsure what kind of trader I should be. Should I scalp, day trade, swing, or invest?"

Pro: "Good. That's a question every evolving trader faces. Each path can be profitable, if it matches your mind, not just your ambition."

The Four Trading Archetypes

FACTOR	SCALPER	DAY TRADER	SWING TRADER	INVESTOR
Holding Period	Seconds to minutes	Minutes to hours	Days to weeks	Months to years
Goal / Objective	Small, quick profits	Capture intraday moves	Profit from short to medium trends	Long-term wealth creation
Primary Edge	Speed and execution	Intraday price action	Trend alignment & technical levels	Fundamental value
Emotional Demand	Very high	High (concentration)	Moderate (patience)	Low (discipline)
Decision Speed	Instant	Fast	Measured	Very slow
Market Focus	Micro movements	Intraday volatility	Short to medium term trends	Macro fundamentals

Pro: "There's no superior style, only the one that keeps you sane. Investing should be done by all"

"Everyone should be an investor in some means. Compounding of long-term wealth cannot be skipped or missed by retail traders."

Various Trading Styles

Trading Style	Metaphor / Mindset	Holding Period	Core Pros	Core Cons
Scalper	**Flying a Jet.** Fast mind, faster trade. Thrive on discipline, not dopamine.	Seconds to Minutes	Frequent setups, minimal overnight exposure, quick feedback loops.	Emotionally exhausting, high transaction costs, tiny margin for error.
Day Trader	**Surfing the Day's Tide.** Riding the wave and stepping off before it crashes."	Minutes to Hours	Controlled daily routine, no overnight risk, multiple opportunities.	Prone to overtrading, emotionally draining, requires structured time blocks.
Swing Trader	**Road Trip.** Slower, steadier, but you enjoy the view. Offers space to think and live.	Days to Weeks	Less screen time, higher reward per trade, emotionally sustainable.	Requires patience, prone to PnL swings & overnight volatility, demands conviction in analysis.
Investor	**Marathon Mindset.** Art of letting compounding do the heavy lifting. Seek transformation, not thrill.	Months to Years	Stress-free wealth creation, lower taxes and transaction costs, works alongside other careers.	Demands deep patience, hard to ignore market noise, feels too slow for action seekers.

The Illusion of Speed

Pro: "Most traders start with speed because it feels like progress. But speed without skill multiplies mistakes.

- Scalping is a bike race,
- Day trading is a car drive,
- Swing trading is a long road trip,
- Investing is a train journey.

Each one reaches if you stay on track."

"The faster your trading style, the slower your mind must become."

Final Reflection

Amateur: "So I don't have to trade the way others do, just in the way I can manage best."
Pro: "Exactly.
The market doesn't care about speed, only about survival.
Choose peace over pace, and profit will follow."

Chapter Summary

- Scalping = precision and pressure; high reward, high fatigue.
- Day trading = rhythm and repetition; requires energy management.
- Swing trading = balance between time and reward.
- Investing = compounding through patience.
- Match your trading style to your temperament, not temptation.
- Speed creates thrill; patience creates freedom.

4.5 AVERAGING, PYRAMIDING & THE ILLUSION OF SPEED

"The Thin Line Between Mastery and Mayhem"

Opening Scene

Amateur: "Pro, now that I know my trading style, there's something else I've been doing, averaging my positions when they go against me. It works most of the time… but when it doesn't, I lose big."

Pro: "That's because you're playing probability without protection. Averaging works until it destroys the math."

The Truth About Averaging

Pro: "Averaging down is the illusion of control. It wins small and often, and then loses huge and rarely."

Trade #	Result	Cumulative P/L
1–8	Small Wins	+$8,000
9	Averaged Loss	–$15,000
10	Averaged Loss	–$15,000
Net Result		**–$22,000**

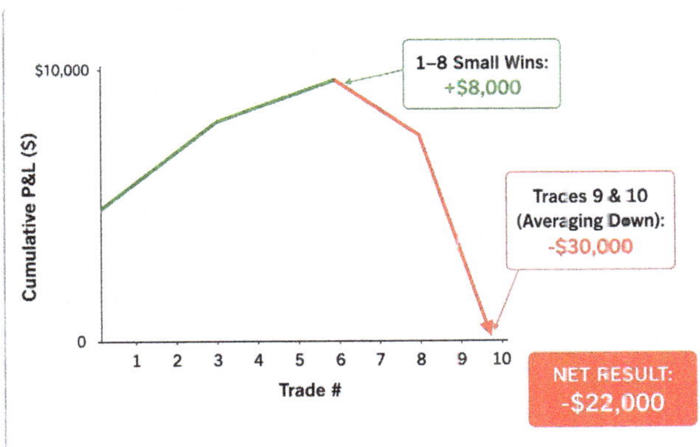

Pro: "The same strategy that made you confident becomes the one that breaks you."

Why Averaging Feels Right

Pro: "Averaging appeals to ego, it whispers, 'You can't be that wrong.' It replaces acceptance with arrogance."

Amateur: "So even when it works, I'm teaching myself the wrong habit?"
Pro: "Exactly. You're reinforcing denial."

The Mathematics of Self-Destruction

Pro: "If you risk 1% and add two more times, your real exposure is now 3–4%. You've tripled risk to defend a wrong idea."

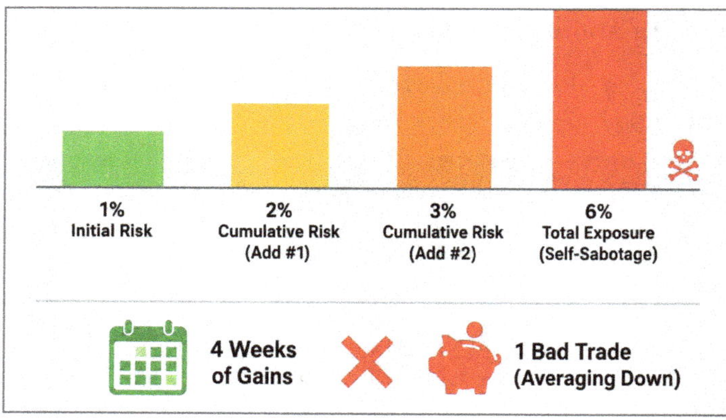

Pro: "One bad trade can erase four weeks of good trading. That's not strategy; that's self-sabotage."

Why Averaging Is a Sin

Pro: "Averaging is a sin because it trains you to reject reality. It punishes humility and rewards hope, until it reverses."

"Averaging is ego disguised as strategy."

Pro: "The truth is, it's not about saving a trade. It's about saving face."

The Discipline of Pyramiding

Amateur: "So, when is it okay to add to a position?"
Pro: "When you're adding to strength, not weakness; that's pyramiding."
He explained with calm precision:

"If your first trade risks 1% and moves +1R in your favour, you add another position while moving your stop to breakeven. Your total risk stays 1%, but your reward doubles."

Stage	Position	Risk	Total Exposure
Entry 1	1%	1R	1%
Add at +1R	+1%	0 (stop moved)	1%
Target	3R	-	3× reward

Pro: "That's how professionals add, not through hope, but through proof."

Pro (continued): "<u>It doesn't mean you add to every winner</u>. Each addition needs confirmation: structure, momentum, and an updated stop-loss so your **total initial risk remains the same.**
Don't fear if a trade ends as a small loss or breakeven instead of a big winner. The process handles the small losses and builds the path to the rare, large profits."

The Illusion of Speed

Pro: "Averaging lures you because it gives the illusion of control. Pyramiding seduces you because it feels like mastery. Both become dangerous when risk is not contained. Speed, size, and overconfidence all grow from the same seed: **impatience.**
When you manage risk, speed serves you; when you don't, it betrays you."

"In pyramiding, half the trades might settle at breakeven or small losses. But the few that run, the true big winners, they pay for everything else. Never forget the four quadrants: it's the **top-right box- the big winners** that builds empires."

"Averaging feeds ego.
Pyramiding rewards discipline.
Only risk control keeps both from killing you."

Final Reflection

Amateur: "So being wrong isn't the problem; refusing to admit it is."
Pro: "Exactly. The best traders lose small, not because they're smarter, but because they stop lying to themselves faster."

Chapter Summary

- Averaging down wins often but kills rarely, and fatally.
- It rewires ego to deny reality.
- Pyramiding is adding to strength, not rescuing weakness.
- Risk control is the constant that makes both meaningful.
- Avoiding ruin is the first step toward mastery.

4.6 THE EXIT BLUEPRINT: STOP-LOSS, TARGETS & TRAILING

"Mastering the Art of Leaving the Market Wisely"

Opening Scene

Amateur: "Pro, I've studied entries for months, confirmation, patterns, indicators. But I still end up giving back my profits."

Pro: "That's because your exit is emotional, not intentional.
Most traders prepare for entry, professionals prepare for exit."

The Most Ignored Skill in Trading

Pro: "Everyone talks about setups, entries, and confluences.
Few talks about exits, because exits are harder. Entries give hope; exits demand humility. You can control where you get in, but the market controls how it moves after that. The only real control you have is when and how you choose to get out."

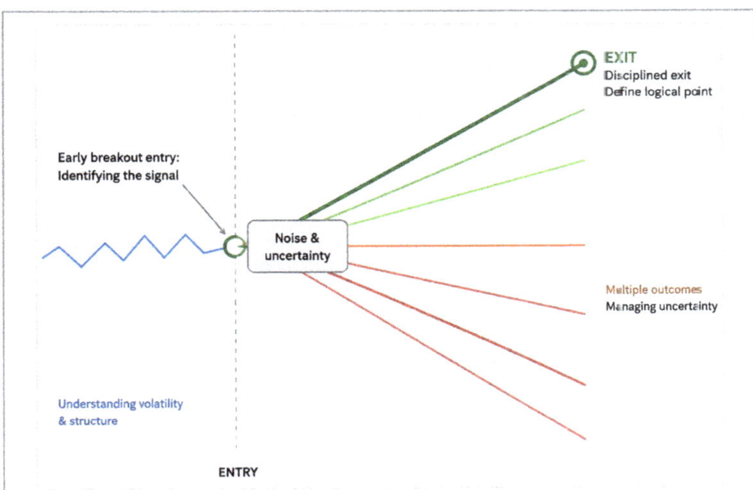

The Myth of "Obvious" Stop-Losses

Pro: "Most traders place their stop-losses at obvious levels, right below swing lows or above resistance. **That's where liquidity lives.** You're literally placing your exit where the market needs your order."

"The market hunts liquidity, not individuals. So don't gift your stop-loss to the crowd."

"Stops should hide behind logic, not visibility."

Stop-Loss Placement Principles

Stop Type	When to Use	Purpose
Structure-Based SL	Around invalidation of your thesis (not candle lows)	Logical stop
Volatility-Based SL	Using ATR or average candle range	Adaptive stop
Time-Based SL	When a trade goes nowhere beyond expected time	Protection against dead trades

Pro: "A good stop isn't where it feels safe; it's where your reason for entry dies."

The Risk–Reward Trap

Pro: "New traders worship the 1:2 ratio and forget that the market doesn't know your math."

"If the nearest logical target gives 1.8R, take it. Don't hold out for 2R just because your calculator said so. Blind mathematics kills practical probability. Trading isn't about ideal numbers; it's about sensible exits."

"Rule: Take profit where the market offers reason, not where your ego demands symmetry."

Partial Exits and Scaling Out

Pro: "One of the smartest habits is partial profit-taking. Book 50–70% at the logical target, then trail the rest for bonus potential."

"This creates balance: emotional release + logical continuation."

Phase	Action	Benefit
TP hit	Book 50–70%	Lock profits
Move SL to BE	Protect equity	Free trade
Trail remainder	Ride extra move	Catch extended run

"Pro Tip: Partial exits turn uncertainty into opportunity."

Trailing Stop Methods

Pro: "Trailing isn't guesswork, it's structure in motion."

Method	How It Works	When to Use
Swing Trail	Move SL behind recent swing highs/lows	Trending markets
EMA Trail	SL behind 9 EMA or 20 EMA	Smooth trends
Fixed Buffer Trail	Lock profits every +1R beyond TP	Volatile phases
Session Trail	Adjust based on session volatility	Intraday setups

Pro: "Trail intelligently, never tighter than logic allows, never looser than your rules permit. Also, always give time and space for the market to move to TP, in that journey, it might retrace, pullback etc but don't tightly trail and getting trailing SL hit early before TP"

Rule of Thumb: Lock reward only after market gives it, not before it earns it.

When to Exit Fully

Pro: "If market reaches a higher time-frame level, or structure looks exhausted, it's wise to close 80–85% and step aside.

You don't always need to squeeze the last drop, the next clean setup will come, and your focus will be fresh.

Professional traders don't chase every candle; they protect every edge."

Predefining the Exit Plan

Pro: "The most dangerous time for a trader is during the trade, because logic fades and emotion take over.

Define your exits before entry.

- Where you'll exit if wrong.
- Where you'll take profit.
- How you'll trail if it goes in your favour."

Once you're in the trade, your only job is to execute that plan, not rethink it."

"Golden Rule: Never decide inside the trade what you could've decided before it. ***Entries create excitement. Exits create equity."***

Final Reflection

Amateur: "So the real skill isn't entering the trade, it's knowing when and how to leave."
Pro: "Exactly. Every trader learns entries. Few master exits, and that's why few stay profitable."

Chapter Summary

- Stop-losses should protect logic, not comfort.
- Avoid obvious SL zones, they're liquidity traps.
- Don't chase textbook RR; take sensible exits.
- Partial exits balance psychology and profit.
- Trail logically using structure or EMA.
- Define your exit plan before you click buy or sell.
- Exits build longevity, not entries.

4.7 ATTENTION, STIMULATION & THE ART OF WAITING

"Why divided focus quietly destroys good traders"

Opening Confession

Amateur: "Pro, I need to admit something honestly.

Over the last three years, as I learned about focus, discipline, consistency, deep work, distraction-free environments, and the power of daily baby steps…I realised something uncomfortable.

I only gave myself **50 to 70% effort** in trading and even in entrepreneurship."

He paused, choosing his words carefully.

"Not because I didn't care. Not because I was lazy. But because most of my struggle came down to one thing. He looked at the screen."

"**Waiting.**"

The Real Struggle

Amateur: "In trading, the hardest part isn't analysis. It's **waiting** for a trade and after entering, waiting for it to develop. We can't just stare at the chart doing nothing. But when we try to do something else, reading a book, watching a podcast, back testing, we can't give full attention to that either.

The market is always ticking. So, part of my mind stays glued to the chart."

He continued.

"If I focus on learning, I execute a trade with only 50 percent attention. If I back test, I feel like I'm missing live market action. And eventually, I doom scroll.

So, I'm not fully trading. I'm not fully learning. I'm not fully resting. I'm just divided."

Pro's Diagnosis

Pro: "What you're describing isn't lack of discipline. It's **divided attention**. Most traders fail not because they don't know enough, but because they cannot tolerate waiting without **stimulation**. You weren't underperforming because of low effort. You were underperforming because your attention was constantly split."

Trading Is Mostly Waiting, Not Doing

Pro: "Trading punishes action-oriented minds. You wait for the setup. You wait for execution.
You wait for outcome. The hardest part isn't analysis. The hardest part is doing nothing without leaking attention. Most traders cannot tolerate that void."

"Trading punishes action-oriented minds.
The hardest part is doing nothing without leaking attention.

Divided Attention Is the Silent Killer

Pro: "When you wait for a trade while reading, watching, or scrolling…You are not trading. You are not learning. You are fragmenting cognition.

This creates:

- shallow thinking
- impulsive entries
- emotional exits
- mental fatigue disguised as productivity

And the worst part? You feel busy, so you feel productive."

Market Presence Creates False Urgency

Pro: "The market is always ticking and that's a psychological trap. The brain interprets:

- moving candles

- price noise
- constant updates

As something requiring response, even when your system says wait.
So, you act impulsively.
Or you distract yourself. Both are the same failure."

The Deeper Truth: Mode Confusion

Pro: "Your real problem was never effort. It was **mode confusion**. You mixed:

- trading mode
- learning mode
- waiting mode
- living mode

inside the same hours, same room, same screen. The brain cannot switch cleanly under those conditions.
So, you lived at 50 to 70 percent capacity. This is not a character flaw.
It's a **design flaw**.

The Correct Mental Model for Trading

Pro: "Trading has only **three valid states**." "Anything else is noise.

State 1: Execution-Ready

- Setup imminent
- Alerts active
- Full attention
- No books
- No videos
- No phone

You either stare at the chart or you walk away. Nothing in between.

State 2: Waiting Without Stimulation

This is where most traders fail. Rules:

- Charts minimized or alerts only
- Leave the desk

- Low-stimulation activities only
    - walking
    - stretching
    - light chores

No learning. No content. No scrolling. Waiting is an action.

<u>State 3: Learning and Review</u>

Market closed or you are fully flat. Only then:

- back testing
- journaling
- reading
- podcasts

Never during live market.

One Rule That Changes Everything

Pro: "Never combine trading with intellectual consumption. Reading while waiting is not productive.
It is attention theft. The brain stays half in the market and half in the content, so neither consolidates. This is why capable traders feel stuck for years."

"Why do capable traders remain stuck for years? Because they mix execution with consumption. They trade while simultaneously consuming content & their brain splits its focus. Half of it is in the market, reacting to price. The other half is processing ideas, opinions, strategies or analysis from outside."

Why Doom Scrolling Happens

Pro: "Doom scrolling is not a habit. It is relief from unresolved attention tension. You were not trading, not learning, not resting. So, the brain chose stimulation. Remove the tension, and scrolling disappears naturally."

The Practical Shift

Amateur: So, what is the ideal practical shift needed?

Pro: "Replace watching with **alert-based living**."

Rules:

- define exact setup conditions
- set alerts or checklist system.
- leave the screen
- live your life until the alert calls you back or checklist conditions are right.

"If there is no alert or ticks in checklist, there is no trade. If there is no trade, there is no market. This single rule restores full attention to both trading and life. Professionals are not present all the time. They are present only when required.

"If there is no trade alert or ticks in checklist, there is no trade. If there is no trade, there is no market."

Final Reflection

Amateur: "So I didn't fail because I lacked discipline."

Pro: "No. You failed because you tried to be present everywhere. Professionals protect their attention. You are not late to this realization. You are early."

Chapter Summary

- Trading is a waiting game, not an action game
- Divided attention destroys execution quality
- Market noise creates false urgency
- Mode confusion causes long-term stagnation
- Waiting without stimulation is a skill
- Alerts or checklist restore clarity and peace
- Attention, not effort, is the real edge

4.8 DISCIPLINE, CHALLENGES & SHARPENING THE AXE

"Why the best traders trade less"

Opening Scene

Amateur: "Pro, I've realised something. Most of my improvement didn't come from taking more trades. It came from stepping back and fixing myself. I feel like I spent years swinging the axe… and very little time sharpening it."

The Woodcutter's Truth

Pro: "That analogy is perfect. A woodcutter doesn't cut all day. He sharpens his axe most of the time. In trading, **less action produces better outcomes**. You don't need to trade every day. You don't need to trade every session. You don't need to be active all the time. You need patience to wait for the trade. And patience to wait for the trade to finish."

Why Traders Break Their Own Rules

Amateur: "Many traders say things like 'I knew the trade would hit my target, but I exited midway.'
Or 'My rule was to trail using EMAs or price action, but I exited after seeing good P&L.'
Why does this keep happening?"

Pro: "Because rules on paper mean nothing if discipline isn't trained in life."

Discipline Starts Outside the Chart

Pro: "My mentor quit smoking after a habit of nearly **15 years**.

The Amateur looked surprised. Pro continued.

"He understood one thing deeply: if you cannot control impulses in life, you will never control them when money is involved. That discipline didn't just change his health. It changed his trading. When money fluctuates, your nervous system takes over. Whatever control you trained in life shows up instantly."

The Real Problem Behind Early Exits

Pro: "You didn't exit early because the market changed. You exited because **you changed**. Breaking exit rules, trailing rules, or staring at P&L is not a strategy problem. It's an **impulse regulation problem**. Discipline is not intelligence. It is repetition under pressure."

The Challenge Framework:

Amateur:" how to Train myself for better discipline. I understand it's a muscle."

Pro: "You don't fix everything at once. You fix **one weakness at a time**, for **30 days**, without negotiation. No profit judgement. Only rule obedience.

Many traders say their exit plan is structured: Book 50 percent at TP1 and trail the remaining 50 percent.

But when the moment comes, most close 100 percent at TP1. Or worse, they exit even before TP1.

Why?

Because when price hits target, emotions spike. Relief feels safer than discipline.

Yes, sometimes the trailed portion comes back to breakeven. It feels painful to watch open profit disappear.
It feels like wasted money.

But here is the truth: The trade that defines your month is rarely the first partial exit. It is the one that trends.
The one that runs. The one that you only capture because you respected your trailing rule.

If your rule says, your profit booking plan is

- 50 percent at TP1
- 50 percent trail

Then that is the rule. Not 100 percent at TP1. Not 70 percent. Not "today feels volatile, let me just close."

Rules are not suggestions. They are the edge.

Consistency in execution is what allows the statistical outlier to pay you. Break the rule once, and you train your brain to negotiate with discipline.

Follow the plan when it is uncomfortable. Especially when it is uncomfortable.

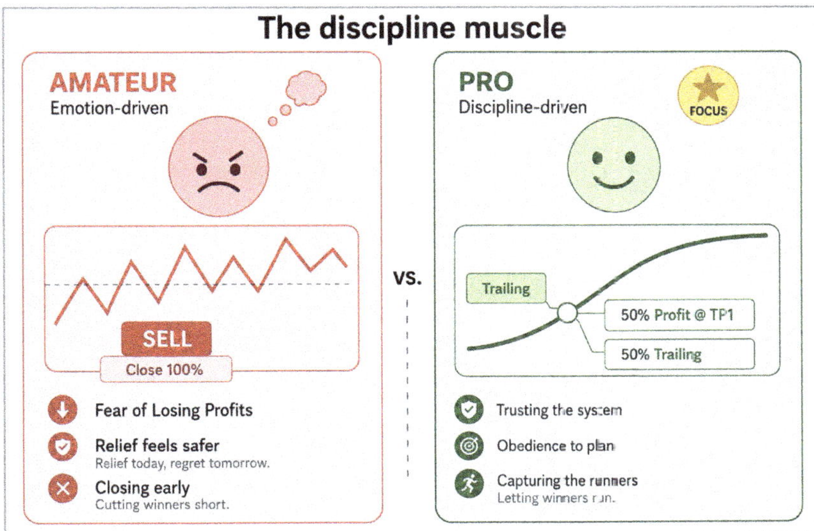

Because in trading, the difference between average and exceptional is not intelligence. It is obedience to your own system.

How the Challenge System Works

- One rule
- One month
- No exceptions
- Success = following the rule, not making money

Challenges don't change markets. They change **you**. Give yourself lot of challenges. Improve your brain muscles. Readers can choose 12 or extend to 15 months. Below are various challenges they could take up and improve their discipline."

Month	Challenge	Purpose
1	Trade only **one session**	Kill overtrading
2	**Set & Forget** trades	Train trust
3	**No P&L checking** during trades	Remove emotional exits
4	Same **risk per trade** entire month	Build consistency
5	Exit only at **planned TP or SL**	Eliminate mid-way exits
6	Trail only using **predefined method**	Stop panic exits
7	No revenge trades	Emotional reset
8	Hard daily stop (eg. 2%)	Capital protection
9	Fixed **pre-market routine**	Execution readiness
10	No phone or distractions during trades	Full presence
11	Skip trades if criteria not met	Selectivity
12	Trade fewer days, review more	Quality over quantity
13	Fixed wake-up time	Nervous system stability
14	Exercise minimum 4–5 days/week	Emotional regulation
15	No late meals before sleep	Cognitive clarity

The Non-Negotiables: Standards that never change

Amateur: "If challenges rotate, what stays constant?"

Pro: "Foundations don't rotate. These are **non-negotiable**.

Markets shift. Volatility expands and contracts. Win rates fluctuate. But professional standards do not move. These are the Trader's Non-Negotiables.

I. Documentation Is Mandatory

1. Journal Every Trade

Every trade must include:

- Entry reason
- Stop logic
- Target logic
- Emotional state at execution

If it is not written, it did not happen. Memory edits reality. Writing preserves truth.

2. Weekly Trade Review

You do not improve while trading. You improve while reviewing. Every week:

- Identify execution mistakes
- Spot recurring patterns
- Track emotional leaks

Performance evolves in reflection, not reaction.

3. Weekly Back testing or Replay

- Reinforce patience
- Study missed opportunities
- Strengthen trust in your edge

Back testing sharpens the axe. Live trading swings it.

II. Risk Is Sacred

4. Fixed Risk Per Trade

- No increase after wins
- No reduction after losses

When risk changes, psychology breaks. Consistency in risk creates stability in mind.

5. Hard Drawdown Rules

Define them before you ever need them:

- Daily stop
- Weekly stop
- Emotional stop

These rules do not limit profit. They limit damage. Survival precedes growth.

III. Process Before Outcome

6. Process Before P&L

Judge yourself on execution quality, not monetary outcome. A well-executed losing trade is success. A poorly executed winning trade is failure.

7. P&L Is Feedback, Not a Command

Profit and loss inform you. They do not control you. They are data. Not instructions.

IV. Execution Integrity

8. No Rule Changes Mid-Trade

If the rule changes during the trade, it was never a rule. It was emotion.

9. Rules Are Decided Before Entry, Not During Emotion

All decisions are made in clarity. None are made in heat.

10. Respect Market Absence

Flat is a position. No trade is a strategic choice. Remember, no trade is a good trade.

11. No Trade Is a Valid Outcome

The market does not reward activity. It rewards precision. Participation is optional. Discipline is not.

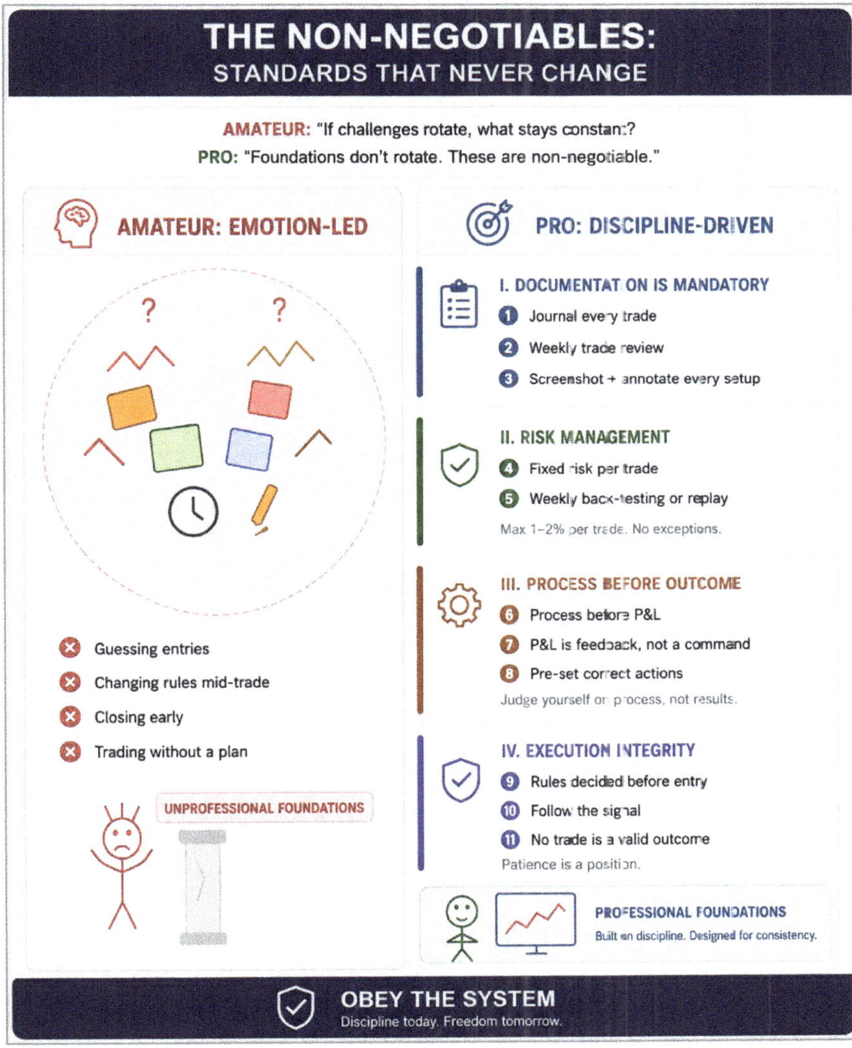
THE NON-NEGOTIABLES:
STANDARDS THAT NEVER CHANGE
AMATEUR: "If challenges rotate, what stays constant?
PRO: "Foundations don't rotate. These are non-negotiable."
AMATEUR: EMOTION-LED
?
?
Guessing entries
Changing rules mid-trade
Closing early
Trading without a plan
UNPROFESSIONAL FOUNDATIONS
PRO: DISCIPLINE-DRIVEN
I. DOCUMENTATION IS MANDATORY
1 Journal every trade
2 Weekly trade review
3 Screenshot + annotate every setup
II. RISK MANAGEMENT
4 Fixed risk per trade
5 Weekly back-testing or replay
Max 1–2% per trade. No exceptions.
III. PROCESS BEFORE OUTCOME
6 Process before P&L
7 P&L is feedback, not a command
8 Pre-set correct actions
Judge yourself on process, not results.
IV. EXECUTION INTEGRITY
9 Rules decided before entry
10 Follow the signal
11 No trade is a valid outcome
Patience is a position.
PROFESSIONAL FOUNDATIONS
Built on discipline. Designed for consistency.
OBEY THE SYSTEM
Discipline today. Freedom tomorrow.

To summarize the core non-negotiables, below is the table

#	Standard	Core Rule	Why It Exists
1	Journal Every Trade	Entry, Stop, Target, Emotion must be written	Writing removes self deception
2	Weekly Review	Identify mistakes and emotional leaks	Growth happens in review, not execution
3	Weekly Backtesting	Study missed and valid setups	Reinforces patience and confidence
4	Fixed Risk Per Trade	No increase after wins. No reduction after losses	Stable risk = stable psychology
5	Hard Drawdown Rules	Daily, Weekly, Emotional stops defined	Limits damage before ego takes over
6	Process Before P&L	Judge execution, not outcome	Protects long term edge
7	P&L Is Feedback	Data, not instruction	Prevents emotional decisions
8	No Mid Trade Rule Changes	Rules are fixed before entry	Stops emotional improvisation
9	Pre Defined Trade Plan	Decisions made in clarity	Emotion cannot design structure
10	Respect Market Absence	Flat is a position	Prevents forced trades
11	No Trade Is Valid	Participation is optional	Protects capital and psychology

Pro: "Foundations do not rotate with conditions. Standards that bend under pressure were never standards. These are not preferences. They are survival requirements."

How Challenges and Non-Negotiables Work Together

Pro: "Challenges build muscles. Non-negotiables protect bones. You can change how you train. You never break the skeleton."

> *"If you can't follow rules when nothing is at stake, you won't follow them when money is on the line."*

Final Reflection

Amateur: "So trading isn't about winning trades."

Pro: "No. It's about winning **days of discipline**. When you sharpen your axe daily, cutting becomes effortless."

Chapter Summary

- Less trading leads to better outcomes
- Preparation beats activity
- Discipline outside trading reflects inside trading
- One-month challenges build self-control
- non-negotiables protect consistency
- Life habits shape trading behaviour
- Obedience precedes profitability

PART 5: TRADING PHILOSOPHY

"You don't conquer the market.
You learn to move in rhythm with it."

5.1 THE LONELINESS TRAP

"When Freedom Becomes Isolation"

Opening Scene

Amateur: "Pro, this is why I love trading.

- No boss.
- No traffic.
- No office politics.
- No meetings.
- No dressing up.
- No dealing with difficult people.

Just me and the charts. Isn't this the perfect career?"

Pro smiled. "It's perfect… until it isn't."

The Attractive Side of Solitude

Pro: "Trading offers a kind of freedom most careers don't.

- You control your time
- You avoid toxic environments
- You eliminate unnecessary social noise
- You reduce energy drain from workplace drama

For many, that alone feels like success."

Amateur nodded. "I don't have to iron shirts. I don't have to commute. I don't have to answer to anyone."

Pro: "Yes. But remember something important. Humans are social creatures.
Not machines."

The Hidden Cost of Screen-Only Living

Pro: "When you trade full-time, your world shrinks quietly."

- One room
- One screen
- One chair
- One set of charts

"At first, it feels peaceful. Then it becomes repetitive. Then it becomes isolating.

Years pass. Friends move on. Colleagues disappear. Children grow up. Your social circle narrows. Eventually, it's just you and volatility."

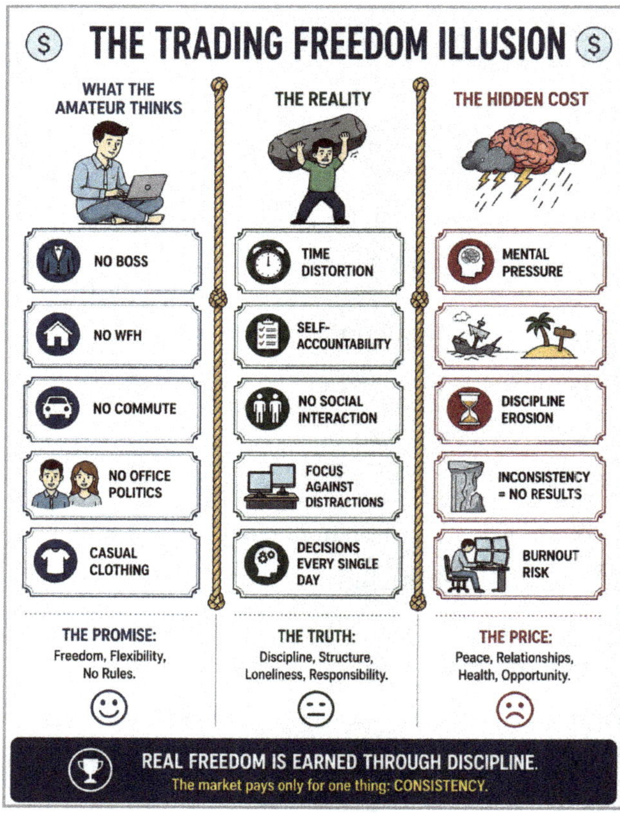

The Psychological Impact

Pro: "Loneliness in trading creates silent problems:

- Over-attachment to outcomes
- Emotional amplification
- Mood swings tied to PnL
- Lack of external perspective
- Identity merging with performance

When the market is green, you feel alive. When the market is red, you feel worthless.

Why?

Because the market became your only interaction."

The Myth: "I Don't Need People"

Amateur: "But I don't like dealing with people. Trading feels clean."

Pro: "You cannot escape people.

Even as a trader, you still deal with: Your partner, children, parents, community, Society

Avoiding strangers does not remove human interaction. It only reduces variety. Isolation does not equal independence."

The Long Career Problem

Pro: "Trading is not a one-year sprint. It's a decades-long path. If your only stimulation is market movement, your nervous system becomes dependent on volatility. Then, boredom becomes intolerable. Silence becomes uncomfortable. Weekends feel empty.

After three or four years, many traders feel stuck. Not financially. Emotionally."

The Retirement Question

Pro: "Ask yourself something uncomfortable. If tomorrow the market closed permanently, who would you be?"

Amateur stayed silent.

Pro: "If your entire identity is 'trader', you built a narrow life.

Money without relationships feels hollow."

The Healthy Model of a Trader's Life

Pro: "Your work may be solitary. But your life should not be."

A balanced trader needs:

1. Physical outlet in the form of gym, Martial arts, running club, Sports league
2. Social engagement like Community group, Business network, Faith circle, Intellectual circles
3. Creative hobbies like Writing, Music, Teaching, Building something
4. Family presence which is most important where it is not distracted presence. Real presence

"Trading should fund your life. Not replace it. Trading should be 1 pillar, not the entire life. "

The Discipline of Designing Your Social Life

Pro: "Just like you design your risk rules, you must design your life structure."

Schedule:

- Weekly social interaction
- Monthly non-trading travel
- Offline hobbies
- Screen-free blocks

"You cannot let the market become your only companion."

A Quiet Truth

Pro: "The traders who burn out fastest are not the ones who lose money.

They are the ones who lose connection. Loneliness makes small drawdowns feel catastrophic. Community makes losses feel manageable."

Final Reflection

Amateur: "So trading isn't about escaping the world?"

Pro: "No. It's about creating space in the world. But space must be filled with life. Pressing buy and sell is not a full existence. Build a life where trading is one pillar. Not the entire structure."

Chapter Summary

- Trading offers freedom, but freedom without balance leads to isolation.
- Humans require social interaction to stay psychologically stable.
- A trader without hobbies becomes emotionally dependent on volatility.
- Identity should not be fully tied to PnL.
- Design your life with the same intention you design your trades.

5.2 TRADING AS PRIMARY INCOME (AND WHY YOU SHOULD WAIT)

"Freedom Without Foundation Is Fragile"

Opening Scene

Amateur: "Pro, I've been consistent for months. I'm thinking of quitting my job to trade full-time."

Pro: "That thought visits every trader. The question isn't can you, it's – **"should you now."**

Trading Is a Business, not a Salary

Pro: "Salaries arrive on schedule; market income doesn't. A business survives lean months because it plans for them. He drew two lines, one smooth, one jagged.

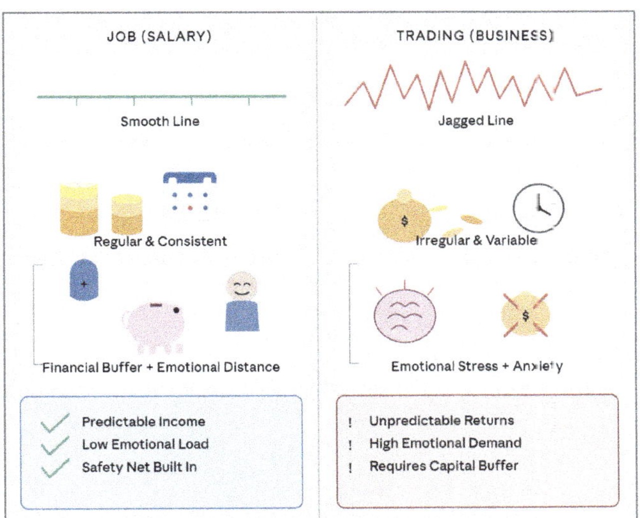

"Until you have a buffer and emotional distance from your bills, trading for income becomes trading for anxiety."

Psychological Dependence

Pro: "When you need the market to pay rent, every tick feels personal. You start forcing setups to feed survival."

Dependency Level	Effect
Low	Freedom → Focus
Medium	Pressure → Impulsiveness
High	Desperation → Destruction

Pro: "You must earn the right to trade for income by first trading for process."

The Bridge Plan

Pro: "Have a bridge, another income stream that pays your peace. Then your trades can grow without emotional rent."

Checklist:

- Maintain 12 months of living expenses.
- Trade part-time until you've done ≥ 2 or 3profitable years.
- Build one steady cashflow side business.

The 100-Day Discipline Challenge

Pro: "Before going full-time, try this."

Rules:

1. Trade 100 days without breaking any process rule.
2. Skip days you're unfit to trade, they don't count.
3. Journal every session honestly.
4. Grade discipline, not profit.

Pro: "If you can complete those 100 days, your emotions are ready even if your capital isn't."

"Financial freedom arrives the day you no longer need the market to feed you."

Final Reflection

Amateur sat quietly for a moment. "So, it's not about confidence… it's about cushion."

Pro nodded. "Exactly. Most traders don't fail because they lack skill. They fail because they put pressure on something that needs patience."

He leaned forward.

"When you depend on trading to survive, every red candle feels like danger. When you trade from stability, every red candle is just data."

"Full-time trading is not an escape from a job. It is a responsibility to yourself."

Amateur smiled slowly. "So, I shouldn't quit to prove I'm serious."

Pro replied, "No. You become serious first. Then quitting becomes unnecessary or obvious."

"Trading is the hardest way to make easiest money"- Said Nithin Kamath

---

Chapter Summary

• Trading income is irregular; expenses are not.
• Psychological pressure increases when trading must pay bills.
• Dependency turns analysis into anxiety.
• A financial buffer creates emotional distance.
• A bridge income protects discipline.
• Complete the 100-Day Discipline Challenge before considering full-time trading.
• Trade for process first. Income becomes a by-product.

5.3 PROP FIRMS: THE MODERN VEHICLE FOR DISCIPLINE AND SCALE

Turning Structure into Freedom

Opening Scene

Amateur: "Pro, I've been trading my personal account for months, but I can't seem to grow it fast enough. I also feel pressured when my own money is at risk."

Pro: "That's the exact reason Prop Firms exist, to give structure, scale, and sanity to serious traders."

Amateur: "But isn't that risky too? They say most traders fail the evaluations."

Pro: "Most fail not because of lack of skill, but because they treat it like a sprint, not a system."

The New Era of Trading Capital

Pro: "In the old days, you needed deep pockets or an institutional seat to manage big money. Today, with Prop Firms, you can access funded capital by proving one thing: discipline. The concept is simple, a firm provides virtual capital once you clear a challenge or evaluation, and in return, they share a percentage of your profit."

Stage	Goal	Requirement
Evaluation Phase 1	Hit profit target (e.g., +8%)	Within drawdown and rule limits
Evaluation Phase 2	Confirm consistency (e.g., +5%)	Maintain discipline and rule compliance
Funded Account	Trade real capital	Follow risk, drawdown, and consistency limits

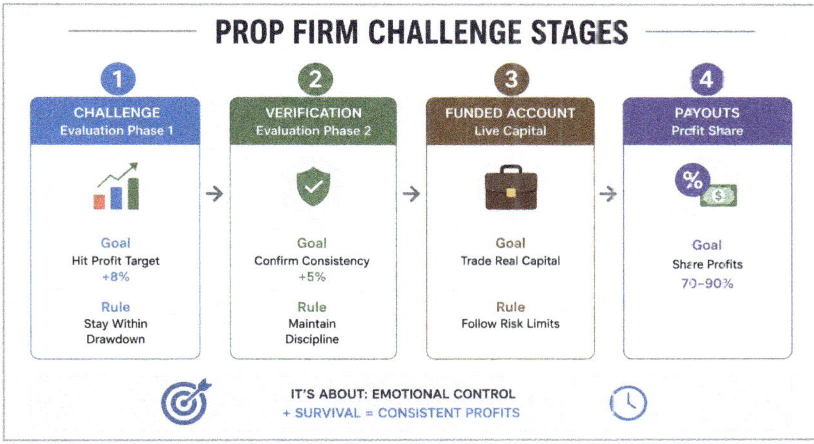

"Passing isn't about luck or performance; it's about proving emotional control. Prop Firms don't look for traders who make money fast; they look for traders who survive long enough to make it consistently. The rules of prop firms vary. Forex prop firms and Futures prop firms have different rules. Also, make sure to use prop firms which has good reviews rather than firms which offer big offers and subsequently vanishes.

A Reality Check on Prop Firms

Pro: "Before you see prop firms as a solution, you must understand their limitations. Not all prop firms are built the same. Some are designed to support traders. Others are designed to eliminate them."

Pro continued: "First, legality varies by country.

In certain regions, including India, trading in CFDs and foreign markets operates in a regulatory grey area or is restricted. Traders must be fully aware of their local regulations before engaging with such platforms."

"Second, the structure itself has limitations. Many prop firms impose strict rules:

- Daily drawdown limits
- Maximum loss caps
- Time-based restrictions likes news trading
- Position holding limitations

These rules may help beginners control risk, but at advanced levels, they can restrict a trader's natural growth."

Amateur: "So even if I become good, the rules can still limit me?"

Pro: "Yes. At some point, a trader needs flexibility, not restriction."

Pro: "Third, there are operational risks. Some firms have a history of:

- Delayed payouts
- Denied profits
- Sudden shutdowns

This is not true for all firms, but it is a reality you must consider."

Pro continued: "The prop firm model itself is built on the assumption that most traders will fail. Evaluation fees are a major revenue source. However, some well-structured firms, especially in futures markets, operate differently. They use trader data, risk models, and in some cases, even replicate successful traders' strategies. These firms are generally more sustainable."

"Choose the firm the way you choose your broker, carefully, critically, and without emotion."

Pro: "Most importantly, understand this: Prop firms are a starting point, not a destination. They are useful when:

- You have limited capital
- You want structured discipline
- You are still developing consistency

But long-term mastery often requires:

- Your own capital
- Your own flexibility
- Your own decision-making freedom"

*"Use prop firms to enter the game.
Don't depend on them to define your career."*

The True Purpose of Prop Firms

Pro: "Most people see Prop Firms as a shortcut to big money. Professionals see them as an external risk manager; a tool to enforce discipline."

Feature	What It Enforces
Daily Drawdown Limit	Emotional Control
Overall Drawdown Limit	Long-Term Survival
Minimum Trading Days	Patience
Consistency Rules	Position Sizing Discipline

Pro: "Every rule that traders hate, is the exact rule that saves them. The firm isn't restricting you; it's protecting you from yourself."

The Psychological Advantage

Amateur: "But Pro, won't these rules feel like pressure?"

Pro: "Pressure comes from ego, not structure. Prop Firms give you a sandbox, a safe boundary where you can practice risk without burning your personal savings. That reduces emotional load, helps you focus on process, and builds psychological resilience. It's ironic, the most disciplined traders often perform better with constraints than with freedom. True traders don't need total freedom; they need intelligent boundaries."

Realistic Returns, Real Results

Pro: "Let's talk numbers, most traders fail because of unrealistic expectations. If you're managing a $100,000 Prop account and aiming for 2–4% monthly growth, that's $2,000–$4,000 in profits. With an 80–

90% payout, you're taking home $1,600–$3,600 per month, without risking your own capital."

Target Type	Monthly Goal	Risk Level	Outcome
Realistic	2–4%	Controlled	Sustainable Growth
Aggressive	10–15%	Moderate	Temporary Growth
Greedy	25–50%	Extreme	Account Death

Pro: "When you aim for 30%+ a month, you're not trading, you're gambling. In trading, survival is success. Compounding comes after survival."

Scaling and Allocation Power

Pro: "Once you're funded and consistent, most firms allow you to scale. You can pass multiple accounts or reach the maximum allocation limit, and suddenly, you're managing hundreds of thousands even millions.

If each account earns just 2–4% per month, multiple accounts or copy setups can multiply your overall returns without increasing your risk.

It's not easy, since every account requires going through the same evaluation process, but it's absolutely worth it. Scaling gives you capital expansion, and the bigger your capital, the greater your opportunity to make steady, conservative returns."

Scaling Path	Capital Access	Approach
Pass one $100k account	$100,000	Foundation
Max Allocation (5–10x)	$500,000–$1,000,000	Scale Capital
Multiple Firm Accounts	$1M+	Scale Diversification
Copy Trading Setup	Cloned across firms	Scale Efficiency

Pro: "The power isn't in trading bigger; it's in managing bigger capital safely. The market doesn't pay you for risking more, it pays you for surviving longer."

Prop Firms as a Discipline Trainer

Pro: "The biggest advantage of Prop Firms isn't money, it's behavioural conditioning. They force you to trade inside limits, respect drawdowns, and keep consistency logs. That structure rewires your mind; it builds the habit of restraint. The moment you start seeing rules as allies, not obstacles, you're ready for real capital. Passing a challenge is easy. Maintaining discipline for months, that's the real test. Remember, Prop firm can be a tool. They are not a guarantee"

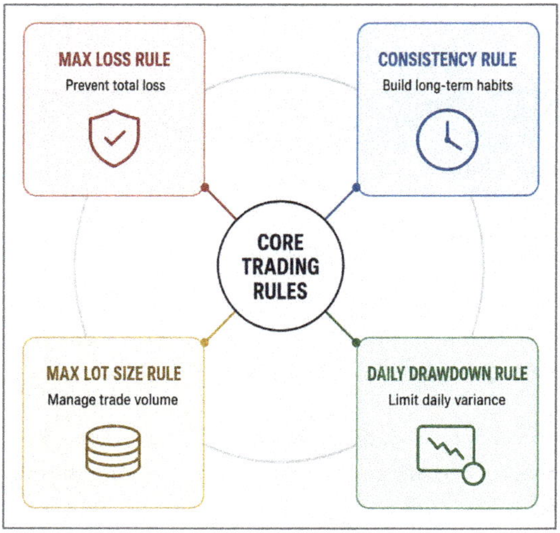

Common Mistakes in Prop Trading

Pro: "Most traders fail for the same emotional reasons that broke their personal accounts."

Pro: "A Prop evaluation exposes who you are, not how good your setup is."

The Prop Firm Mindset

Pro: "Trading a Prop account isn't about 'passing', it's about proving you can be trusted. You're no longer trading your ego; you're trading your reputation.

If you treat a $100k Prop account with respect, one day, you'll earn the right to manage a $1M account with calm.

That's evolution, not scaling by money, but scaling by maturity."

"Prop Firms don't fund traders; they fund discipline."

Final Reflection

Amateur: "So, Prop Firms aren't just a shortcut, they're a structure."
Pro: "Exactly. "

"They filter impulsive traders and reward consistent ones. They're the bridge between independence and institution. If you use Prop Firms as your accountability partner, you'll not only build capital, you'll build character. And in trading, that's the only asset that never faces a drawdown."

Chapter Summary

- Prop Firms provide capital access for disciplined traders.
- Success is defined by control, not aggression.
- 2–4% monthly returns are realistic; 20%+ is ruinous.
- Scaling is about allocation, not leverage.
- Every Prop rule teaches survival, not restriction.
- Treat Prop Firms as structure, not shortcuts.
- Prop Firms fund behaviour, not just performance.

5.4 THE AI ILLUSION

"Speed doesn't replace stability"

Opening Scene

The Amateur leaned back, staring at his screen.

"Pro… AI is everywhere now. It analyses faster, processes more data, even trades automatically."

He paused.

"Will traders even exist in the future?"

The Pro smiled, not surprised.

"That question doesn't come from curiosity. It comes from fear."

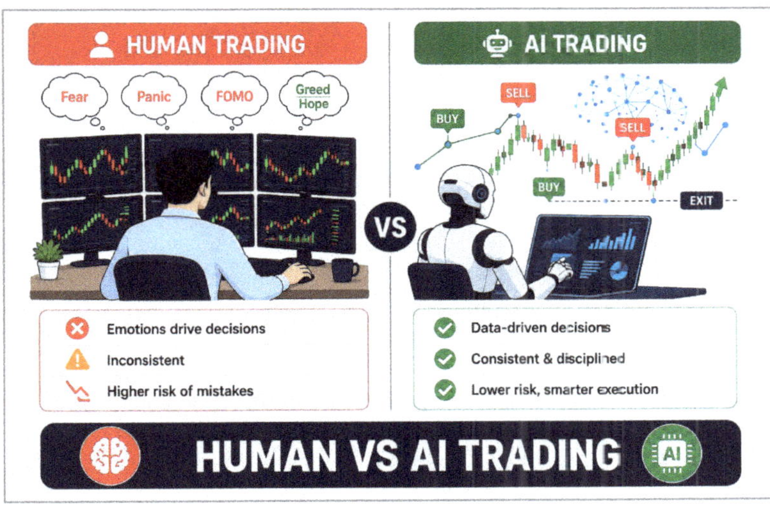

The Shift That's Coming

Pro: "AI will change trading. There is no doubt about that."

He continued calmly.

"It will make analysis faster. Execution sharper. Systems more structured."

He looked at the chart. "But change does not mean replacement."

What AI Can Do

Pro: "Let's be clear. AI is powerful."

- It can analyse massive datasets
- Backtest strategies instantly
- Detect patterns humans miss
- Automate execution
- Reduce mechanical errors

"It will make traders more efficient. But efficiency is not mastery."

The Part AI Cannot Replace

Pro leaned forward.

"The market is not just data. It is behaviour. Every candle on the chart is driven by:

- Fear
- Greed
- Panic
- Hope
- Impulse
- FOMO
- Revenge

As long as humans participate, these emotions will exist. And as long as emotions exist, uncertainty exists."

"AI can process information. It cannot experience pressure."

The Human Pattern You Can't Code

Amateur: "But if AI can process everything faster… won't it eventually understand everything?"

Pro smiled.

"Let me give you a simple example. Have you noticed what happens when a flight lands? The moment the seatbelt sign turns off… people immediately stand up. Even before the aircraft door opens. Even before the queue starts moving. they stand… take their bags… and wait."

He paused.

"Do they reach faster?"

Amateur: "…No."

Pro: "Exactly, they still have to wait for the door to open. They still move in the same line. They still reach the baggage belt at almost the same time."

He continued,

"Now think about boarding. The moment boarding is announced… people rush. Even though everyone knows… the flight won't leave without them. Even if they board last… they still reach the same destination."

He looked at the Amateur.

"Then why do they rush?"

Amateur: "…Impatience?"

Pro: "Emotion. Impulse. Fear of missing out. Need to act."

The Connection to Markets

Pro: "These exact behaviours exist in the market. When price moves fast… traders rush to enter. When price drops… they panic and exit. When others are buying… they feel the need to join. When others are selling… they feel the need to escape. Just like standing early in a flight doesn't get you out faster… Entering emotionally doesn't make you a better trader."

The Deeper Truth

Pro: "As long as humans behave like this. Markets will behave like this. And as long as markets behave like this…AI will never fully replace trading. Because AI can process data. But it cannot feel urgency. It cannot feel fear. It cannot feel the need to act… when doing nothing is the right decision."

***"Markets are not driven by intelligence alone.
They are driven by behaviour."***

The Real Limitation

Amateur: "So AI can't fully control trading?"

Pro: "It can assist. But it cannot decide under emotional uncertainty. You don't lose trades because of lack of data. You lose them because of behaviour."

The Illusion of Intelligence

Pro: "There is another danger. AI doesn't just help traders.
It can mislead them. When something looks intelligent, people assume it is correct. Traders begin to think:

- The model says buy
- The data supports this
- Backtest shows high accuracy

He paused. "But markets are not backtests."

***"AI can give you confidence.
But confidence without context is dangerous."***

History Repeats Itself

Pro: "Every generation believes it has found certainty in the form of Indicators, Strategies, Signals. And now… AI."

He smiled slightly.

"The tool changes. The illusion remains."

Why AI Alone Won't Win

Pro: "Any AI system is built on rules. And markets have a habit of breaking rules. Earlier, traders believed:

- Higher highs = bullish
- Support = buy
- Resistance = sell"

"But what happens today? Liquidity gets taken first. Price moves against the obvious before moving in the actual direction."

The Deeper Truth

Pro: "Markets evolve. What works becomes crowded. And what becomes crowded… stops working."

"AI learns patterns. Markets break patterns."

Where AI Struggles Most

Pro: "AI performs best in structured environments. But markets are not always structured. Especially during:

- News events
- Sudden volatility
- Black swan moves
- Regime shifts

"AI is trained on the past. And markets may punish what worked in the past."

The Hidden Reality

Pro: "Remember this clearly. AI is created by humans. Trained by humans.
Used by humans. It reflects logic. Not emotion. And the biggest mistakes in trading...Don't come from logic. They come from behaviour."

Where AI Actually Helps

Pro: "Use AI as a tool. Not a replacement. It can help you:

- Refine your strategy
- Backtest faster
- Structure your rules
- Improve journaling
- Spot hidden patterns

But it cannot:

- Hold a trade with conviction
- Sit through uncertainty
- Manage fear during drawdown
- Control impulsive behaviour"

"AI can build the system. Only you can execute it."

The Future of Trading

Amateur: "So what does the future look like?"

Pro: "Not AI vs trader. AI + trader. The traders who will win are those who:

- Use AI for speed
- Use experience for direction
- Use discipline for execution"

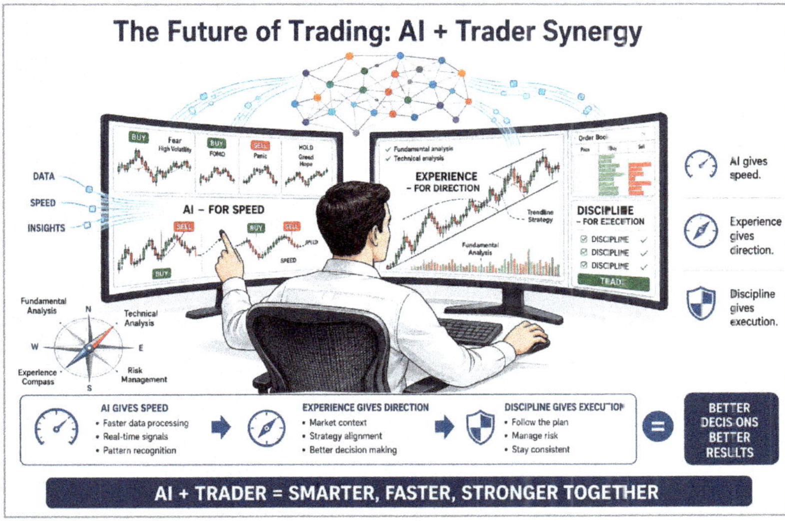

"AI gives speed. Experience gives direction."

The Real Risk

Amateur: "So what should I actually worry about?"

Pro: "Not AI. Your lack of discipline. Most traders are not losing to AI. They are losing to:

- Overtrading
- Impatience
- Emotional exits
- Inconsistency"

A Brutal Truth

Pro: "Most traders are not ready for AI. Because they are not even ready for discipline."

The Final Perspective

Pro: "The market does not reward the fastest. It rewards the most stable. Those who:

- Adapt to change
- Use tools wisely
- Stay disciplined
- Understand behaviour"

Final Reflection

Amateur: "So AI won't replace traders…"

Pro: "No."

He paused.

"But traders who use AI wisely may outperform those who don't. Tools don't make traders. Behaviour does."

Chapter Summary

- AI enhances efficiency, not decision-making
- Markets are driven by human behaviour, not just data
- AI creates confidence, but not context
- Patterns learned by AI can break as markets evolve
- Emotional discipline remains irreplaceable
- The future belongs to hybrid traders: AI + human execution
- The real risk is not AI, but lack of discipline

5.5 THE PARADOX OF TRADING

"Why Even Winning Feels Incomplete"

Opening Scene

Amateur: "Pro, I made my biggest win ever yesterday, but it felt empty. Why?"

Pro: "Because the market rewards progress, not peace. You haven't learned contentment yet."

The Happiness Trap

Pro: "Your brain releases dopamine not when you win, but when you expect to win.
That's why satisfaction fades so quickly, the excitement ends the moment the outcome arrives. The only lasting joy in trading comes from execution, not excitement. Process is peace; prediction is pain."

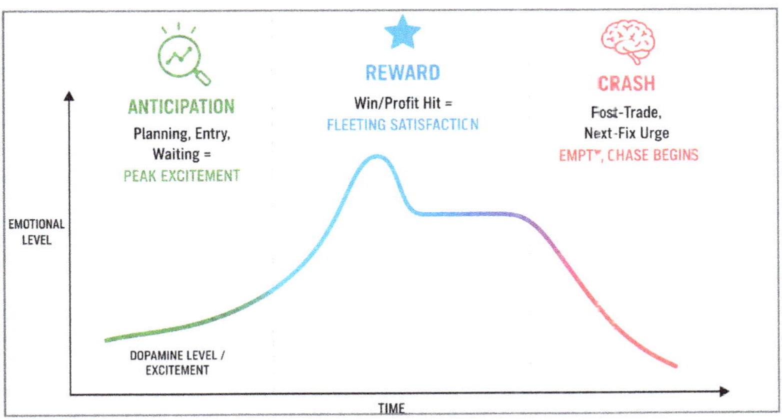

"The only sustainable joy in trading comes from execution, not excitement."

Why a Trader Is Never Happy

Pro: "A trader is almost never happy not because he loses, but because he always imagines a better version of every trade."

- "If he wins, he wishes he had traded larger.
- If he loses, he wishes he hadn't traded at all. Or should have smaller size.
- If his stop-loss hits and price reverses, he regrets not re-entering.
- If his target hits and price keep running, he regrets exiting early.
- If price reverses after hitting his SL, he still wonders if he should've reversed."

"No matter the outcome, the mind finds fault. That's the curse of perfection in a probabilistic game."

Pro: "This endless loop of 'could have, should have' is what keeps traders restless, even when they're right. The market doesn't exhaust you; your mind's rewrites do. You'll keep rewriting the same trade in your head until you learn the real skill, **acceptance.**

Acceptance doesn't mean indifference. It means following your rules, executing your plan, and letting go once the trade is done. That's how peace begins, not after a win, but after acceptance."

Control vs Acceptance

Pro: "Every loss hurts because you think you could've controlled it. But control is an illusion. Process is real. Once you stop arguing with randomness, peace begins.

Control Mindset	Acceptance Mindset
I must be right.	I must follow process.
Fights loss	Learns from loss
Feels helpless	Feels humble
Exhausted	Empowered

"Every loss hurts because you think you could've controlled it.
But control is an illusion. Process is real.

Once you stop arguing with randomness, peace begins."

The Reflection Practice

Pro: "End each week with three questions:"

"Your answers chart your growth more than your P&L."

The Hidden Paradox

Pro: "The market is a mirror. It shows you that satisfaction doesn't come from outcomes. It comes from awareness."

"Most traders think freedom means doing what they want. In truth, freedom comes from not needing the market to make you feel whole.

You can win money and lose peace, that's not winning.
You can lose a trade and still gain clarity, that's growth."

Why Contentment Is the Final Edge

Pro: "At some point, you'll realize trading mastery isn't about controlling the market, it's about controlling your dissatisfaction.

The peace you're looking for doesn't come after a big win. It comes when you no longer need a win to feel peace"

"The market tests your system once a day. It tests your contentment every minute."

Final Reflection

Amateur: "So trading will never make me happy?"

Pro: "Not if happiness depends on the outcome. The market's nature is uncertainty and expecting certainty from it is the root of misery. Your job isn't to eliminate emotion; it's to understand it. Trading will stop hurting the day you stop expecting it to make you happy. Perfection ends the day you realize peace pays more than profit."

Chapter Summary

- Dopamine rewards anticipation, not achievement, that's why wins fade fast.
- Traders stay emotionally dissatisfied because every outcome fuels new "what ifs."
- The mind creates pain by confusing control with influence.
- True growth comes from emotional acceptance, not prediction accuracy.
- Reflect weekly, on your process, not your profit.
- Peace is not the prize, it's the prerequisite for longevity.

5.6 THE MAESTRO LEVEL

"The Stage Where Trades Become Fewer, But Bigger"

Opening Scene

The market was active. Charts were moving. Prices were fluctuating. Opportunities… everywhere. But the Pro wasn't trading.

Amateur (restless): "Pro… the market is moving. Why aren't you taking a trade?"

Pro (calmly): "I am."

Amateur looked confused. "You didn't take anything."

Pro smiled slightly. "I took the decision to wait."

The Shift No One Talks About

Pro: "There is a stage in trading where everything changes."

Amateur: "What changes?"

Pro: "The way you make money."

He continued,

"In the beginning, you survive through discipline. Later, you grow through consistency. But at the highest level… you grow through **conviction.**"

The Truth About Professional Profitability

Pro: "Most traders think professionals make money every day."

He paused.

"That's not true. Even the best traders don't make money from most of their trades. A very small number of trades create the majority of their profits."

Amateur: "So the big trades matter more?"

Pro: "They don't just matter… they define everything."

The Power of Asymmetry

Pro: "Over a year, a trader may take hundreds of trades. But a handful of 'home runs' generate a significant portion of returns. Small trades keep you alive. Big trades build your wealth."

He leaned forward.

"This is where trading becomes asymmetric. One or two exceptional trades can outperform months of normal trading."

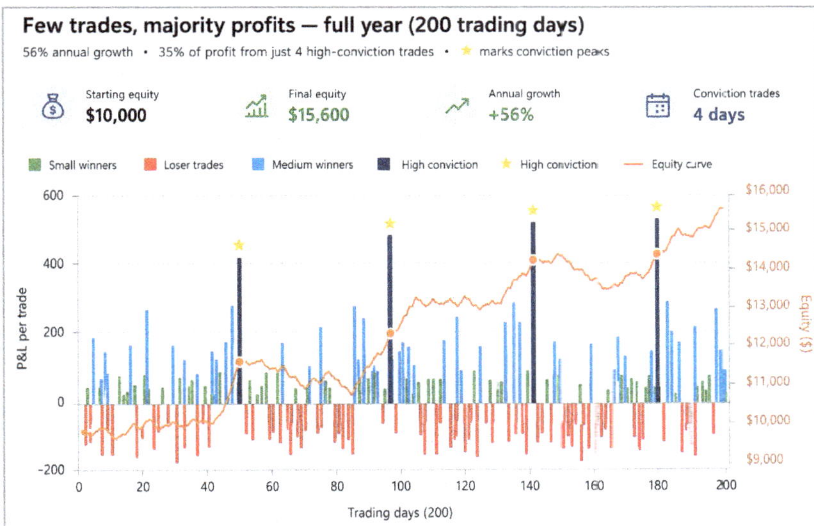

Pro: "There will also be many days with no valid opportunity."

Where These Trades Come From

Amateur: "So these big trades are luck?"

Pro shook his head.

"No. They come from:

- Experience
- Pattern recognition

- Emotional stability
- And most importantly… conviction"

He paused. "Conviction without experience is gambling. Conviction with experience is an edge."

The Mistake Amateurs Make

Amateur: "So should I just hold every trade longer?"

Pro: "That's exactly where amateurs go wrong. You don't blindly hold. You learn to trail intelligently. Not too tight… not too loose. You give the trade room to breathe, but not enough to destroy your gains."

Pro: "Most traders believe big winning trades are luck… or worse, gambling."

He paused.

"That belief is exactly why they never experience them."

Then continued.

"Big trades are not accidents. They are the result of preparation meeting conviction."

The Discipline Behind Conviction

Pro: "At this level, conviction is not emotion. It is structured confidence built on rules. You don't increase size because you feel right. You increase size because your system allows it."

The Concept of Risking Profits

Pro continued: "At this stage, something deeper shifts. You don't risk more from your capital. You expand opportunity from your profits."

Amateur: "What does that mean?"

Pro explained:

"If you've had a strong day or week, a small portion of those profits can be used for high-conviction setups. But understand this clearly…This is not for beginners. This comes only after years of:

- Discipline
- Control
- Consistency

He looked directly at the Amateur. "If you try to jump to this stage without earning it…you won't find conviction. You'll find losses."

The Reality of a Professional Year

Amateur: "Can you compare this with your last financial year?"

Pro nodded. "Good question. I made solid profits last year. But not by trading aggressively every day. Some days, I stayed light. Some days, I didn't trade at all. Some days, I sized up… based on rules, data, and conviction."

He paused.

"And when I reviewed my performance at year-end… 35% of my total profit came from just 4 trading days."

Amateur: "Only 4 days?"

Pro: "Yes. The remaining 65% came from the other ~196 trading days."

He let that sink in. "That's the power of holding winners. If those few big days didn't exist…my entire year would look average."

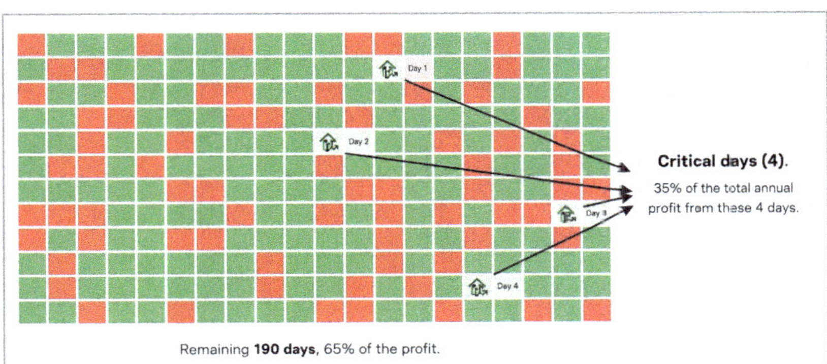

Pro: "Remember, the 4 quadrants? the point here to ensure, we have some big winners, and most importantly not big losers. "

The Patience Premium

Pro: "Most traders are active. Professionals are selective. Amateurs chase trades. Professionals wait."

He continued,

"You are not paid for activity in trading. You are paid for execution… at the right time."

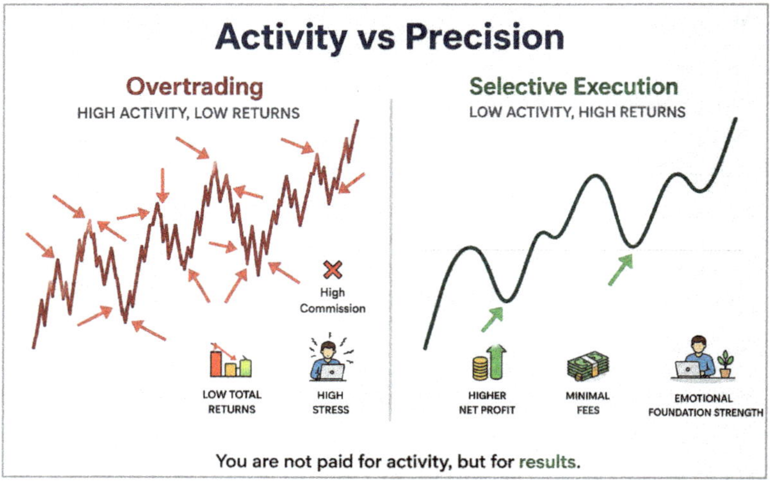

The Emotional Requirement

Pro: "To hold a winning trade, you need something rare. Emotional stability. Because as the trade moves in your favour:

- Fear tells you to exit early
- Greed tells you to overstay
- Ego tells you to interfere"

The professional does something different. He follows the plan."

The Final Truth

Pro: "At the highest level, trading is not about frequency. It's about presence. Being there… when it matters."

Final Reflection

Amateur: "So success in trading isn't about trading more..."

Pro: "It's about missing less of what matters. You don't need more trades. You need better moments."

He paused, then added: "But to operate like this consistently...you don't just need skill. You need a different mindset altogether."

Chapter Summary

- Professionals don't make money from most trades; a few big trades drive results
- Trading becomes asymmetric at higher levels
- Small trades ensure survival; big trades create wealth
- Big winners are not luck; they are a function of preparation, patience and conviction.
- Conviction is built on experience, not emotion
- Intelligent trailing matters more than blind holding
- Position sizing and aggression are rule-based, not impulsive
- Risk expansion comes from profits, not capital
- A few trading days can define an entire year
- Patience and selectivity create the real edge
- This level cannot be rushed; it must be earned

5.7 MINDSET OF A PRO TRADER

Peace Over Perfection

Opening Scene

Amateur: "Pro, you always seem calm. Don't you ever fear losing?"

Pro: "I fear only one thing: losing discipline. Losses don't scare me anymore; impulsiveness does.

The goal isn't to avoid fear, it's to make fear your ally. Fear reminds you that you're risking something real.

It keeps you respectful, not reckless."

Thinking in Probabilities

Pro: "I never think, 'Will this trade win?
I think, 'Does this trade fit my probability framework?'"

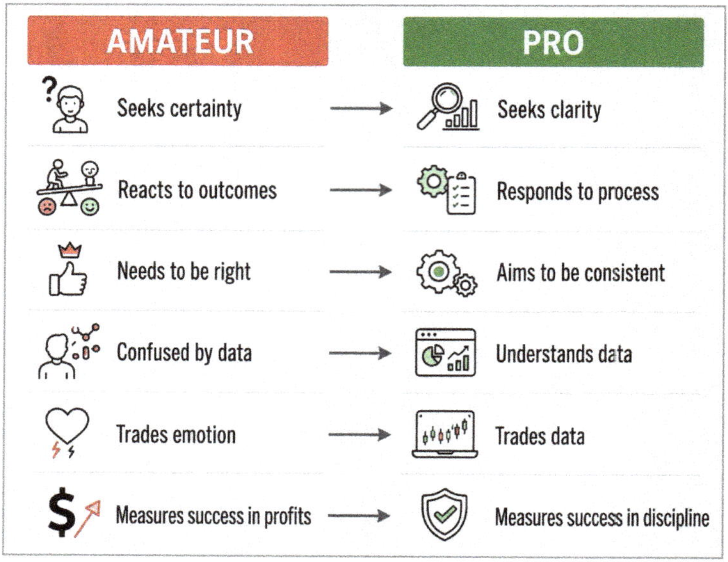

Pro: "A professional doesn't expect to win every trade; he expects to follow every rule. Probability isn't about prediction; it's about endurance."

Stillness as an Edge

Pro: "The rarest skill in trading isn't entry timing, it's stillness. Waiting without restlessness is mastery. Most traders are addicted to action. They equate movement with progress, but in trading, stillness is progress. In stillness, you see structure others miss. You learn to let trades come to you, not chase them."

"No trade is a good trade"

Detachment from Money

Pro: "When you trade money, you become emotional. When you trade process, you become powerful. Money is just a scorecard, not the story. The story is how calmly you played the game."

Amateur: "But isn't money the reason we trade?"

Pro: "At first, yes. Later, it becomes the side effect. You stop chasing money when you start respecting **probability**. That's when the money starts chasing you."

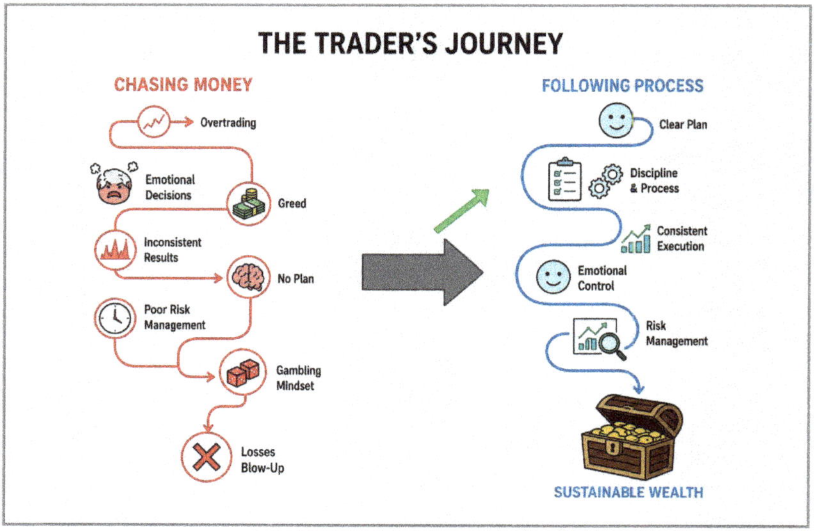

Trading as Life Philosophy

Pro: "Markets mirror life. Risk management teaches boundaries, drawdowns teach humility, and probabilities teach faith."

"A Pro doesn't escape life through trading; he understands life through it.

Because markets, like life, are uncertain, and the only control you have is over yourself."

The Evolution of Emotion

Pro: "The goal isn't to feel nothing. It's to feel everything and still trade well."

"Even after years, emotions don't disappear, fear, greed, hope, doubt, they all return. But mastery isn't their absence; it's your ability to let them pass without reaction."

"You'll know you've evolved when a loss feels like data, a win feels like confirmation, and both feel the same inside."

"Peace isn't found when the market is calm. it's found when you are."

Legacy of a Pro

Amateur: "So the market never changes, only we do."

Pro: "Exactly. The market is constant; chaos wrapped in order. What changes is how you perceive it."

"At first, you fight it. Then you fear it. Then you understand it. And finally, you flow with it."

"That's the real freedom. Not the freedom to trade whenever you want, but the freedom to remain centered, no matter what happens."

Final Reflection

"Trading begins as a pursuit of profit and ends as a practice of peace. You enter to master the market, and leave realizing you were mastering yourself."

Chapter Summary

- Think probabilities, not predictions.
- Stillness is strength; boredom is a hidden edge.
- Money reflects process, not personality.
- Trading is like life: uncertain, humbling, and deeply instructive.
- Emotions don't disappear; they lose control over you.
- Peace isn't perfection, it's presence.

YOU CAME TO MASTER THE MARKET.
YOU'LL STAY TO MASTER YOURSELF.

DISCIPLINE IS YOUR SHIELD.
PATIENCE IS YOUR WEAPON.
PEACE IS YOUR VICTORY.

WIN RATE IS OVERRATED

EPILOGUE: THE JOURNEY NEVER ENDS

Opening Scene

The morning light poured through the window. The Trader sat in silence, just him, his screen, and a cup of coffee that had gone cold.

Charts flickered quietly across the monitors, but he wasn't rushing.

He wasn't scanning for entries or hunting for setups. He was simply observing, detached, aware, peaceful. The same market that once terrified him now looked… calm.

The Trade That Doesn't Need to Be Taken

He saw a perfect setup, clean structure, textbook alignment, all signals confirming. A few years ago, he would have jumped in instantly.

But today, he just smiled.

"Not every opportunity needs action."

He watched the candle move without him, and for the first time in years, he felt no regret.
No FOMO. No urgency. Just quiet respect for the rhythm of the market.

The Inner Dialogue

He whispered softly to himself:

"The market doesn't reward speed, it rewards stillness."
"It doesn't demand perfection, only presence."

He remembered every lesson: The overconfidence after early success. The sleepless nights of drawdowns. The anger after every stop-loss. The endless search for the "perfect strategy." It all seemed distant now, like watching someone else's movie.

The Journal Beside Him

Next to his keyboard sat a worn-out notebook, the same one he started with years ago. Its pages were filled with numbers, scribbles, and quiet realizations.

One note on the last page stood out, written months ago:

"When I stop trying to control the market, I finally learn to control myself."

He smiled reading it, not out of pride, but peace.

The Market's Whisper

The market moved on, as it always does, unpredictable, fluid, indifferent. And for the first time, he didn't feel the need to win against it. Because he finally understood:

"You don't beat the market. You outgrow the version of yourself that tries to."

Reflection

He leaned back in his chair, watching the slow dance of candles on the screen. Every flicker, every move, once chaos, now poetry.

"This is not an end," he thought.
"It's a rhythm I'll keep learning for as long as I live."

He took a slow sip of his coffee. The trade setup that once seemed urgent had already passed. He didn't care. He smiled, the kind of smile that only comes after years of wrestling with your own mind.

The journey never ends, because the market never stops teaching, and the mind never stops learning.

The Closing Words

He turned off his screens. For the first time, the silence of a flat market felt beautiful.

Outside, the world went on, ordinary people chasing certainty in uncertain things.

Inside, he had found what they were all searching for: Not wealth. Not victory. Just peace.

He whispered one last line to himself before leaving the desk:

"The market is not my enemy. It's my mirror.
And I've finally learned to look at it without flinching."

Final Takeaway

Mastery in trading is not about predicting moves, it's about staying unmoved.

The End

WIN RATE IS OVERRATED isn't just a book about markets.

It's a reflection of every trader's inner war, and the quiet, uncelebrated victory that comes when you finally realize that peace is the ultimate profit.

FINAL NOTE: LET'S MAKE TRADING RESPECTABLE AGAIN

Trading today has an image problem; one it doesn't fully deserve. The markets themselves are not the enemy; the people who misuse them are.

The space has become crowded with **scammers, fake mentors, and online frauds**, people who claim they can **time the market perfectly,** who post cherry-picked charts to create illusions of mastery, and who sell signals or courses promising effortless riches.

Even worse, some collect money from others under the pretence of delivering "guaranteed high returns." But let's be honest, if anyone could truly make those returns consistently, they wouldn't need your money.

The truth is, **integrity is a two-way responsibility.**

Yes, there are those who cheat and mislead, but there are also participants who fall for greed, who want shortcuts and believe in "too-good-to-be-true" promises.
Scammers exist because **greed creates an audience for them.**

Let's be fair, this blame doesn't belong to "the market." The market is neutral.
It's not out to fool anyone; it simply reveals what's inside you, your patience, your discipline, your weaknesses, and your choices.

The reputation of trading will only change when **both sides grow up**:

- When educators and influencers teach with honesty instead of hype, and
- When traders and investors learn to question, research, and think before believing.

Most people come into trading with **small capital and big expectations**, they want to multiply money, not manage it. And within months, they lose it all, then blame the market for their pain.

But it doesn't have to be this way. If that same energy was spent on **learning, preserving capital, and understanding psychology**, 90% of those traders wouldn't have quit. They would've evolved.

The first step to becoming a successful trader isn't profit, it's **survival.** Once you survive long enough, the market starts respecting you back. So, let's all be responsible, educators, traders, mentors, and learners alike. Let's rebuild this space with honesty, patience, and process. Let's make trading **respectable** again.

"When you trade responsibly, you don't just protect your capital, you protect the reputation of trading itself."

ABOUT THE AUTHOR

Ajas S
Trader | Cost Management Professional | Author |
Founder, TradeNLeap | Co-Founder, Power of Self

Ajas is a market participant, analytical thinker, and storyteller of discipline. He has been actively trading since 2019 across Indian equities, options, cryptocurrencies, forex, and global futures. Through exposure to euphoric bull runs and brutal drawdowns, he learned that sustainable success in trading is not built on prediction, but on psychology, probability, and process. He views the market as the world's most honest teacher revealing weaknesses without mercy and rewarding patience without bias.

Beyond trading, Ajas is an MRICS-certified Cost Management Professional with over nine years of experience across leading developers, contractors, and consultancies in the UAE and India. He has led multimillion-dollar projects, authored national construction cost research reports for JLL India, and spoken at academic institutions on planning, cost management, and execution strategy. His analytical foundation in cost management naturally shaped his trading philosophy balancing data, discipline, and emotional control.

He holds an MBA in Construction Economics & Quantity Surveying from RICS School of Built Environment, Amity University, a Bachelor's degree in Civil Engineering, and a Certificate in Investment Banking from the New York Institute of Finance.

Ajas founded **TradeNLeap** to share structured insights on trading psychology. He is also the co-founder of **Power of Self**, alongside his wife **Dr. Sana Sainudeen**, a holistic coaching platform focused on mindset, nutrition, and self-mastery.

He continues to trade actively, refine his understanding of market psychology, and share practical lessons on building consistency without emotional burnout. For him, trading is not speculation, it is self-realization.

"The chart is just a mirror. The real market is inside you."

www.ingramcontent.com/pod-product-compliance
Lightning Source LLC
Chambersburg PA
CBHW071339230926
51846CB00002B/389
9789357778664